Acknowledgements

We could not have accomplished our goals without the s[upport] from a number of individuals. First, we would like to thank our [Head of School] George Andrews, who has always supported each of us througho[ut our visit at Saint] Andrew's. We are also fortunate to have the mentoring support of the Associate Head of School, Ann Marie Krejcarek, and the Middle School Head, Mary Ellen Cassini. Thank you, Ann Marie, for your sage advice, comforting assurance, and enthusiasm for our project. The handbook was greatly improved by the learned advice of Mary Ellen Cassini. Your attention to detail helped us delve more deeply into the project as you proofread early versions.

We would like to thank Carmen Ashley for her insight and advice as a reading specialist, Theo Stephenson for her contribution to the section on Life Skills, and Betsy Pickup for her invaluable advice on copyright and legal issues. A special thank you to one of our students, Noah Kimmel, for helping us get started on *Publisher.* It would have taken us forever to complete the tasks before us without his wise counsel. We would like to thank Jackie Gorora (and her ever so patient family) for her help with problems that emerged while working with *Publisher* and other computer-related issues. We appreciate the open-door policy that Lee Munro, SAS's I.T. Support Coordinator, had with us and the technical assistance that Upper School student Terrance Bennett provided. A thank you to Greg Summers, who proofread one of the last versions. We greatly appreciate the time and insights given by Gretchen Steinberg who spent many hours editing and proofreading the final version. It is important to note that those who proofread for us should be relieved of any errors that may remain. This project would not have been completed without the generosity of SAPA (and our SAS parents) for providing funds for the printing of the first two editions for SAS students. We are appreciative of the support and suggestions we received from our colleagues. Finally, we thank our friends, and most importantly, our families who were extremely supportive as we spent countless hours compiling this handbook.

We hope the *Study Skills Tool Kit* will be warmly received and well used. We have made a few revisions since the first printing. During our second revision, we were fortunate to have the talents of Christie Caraballo, who spent part of the summer before her freshman year creating illustrations for us. Her drawings are an amazing contribution to our book! Our humble thanks goes to the faculty and administration at Saint Mark's Episcopal School in Palm Beach Gardens, Florida, who became our first clients, purchasing books for their students.

It must be noted that this handbook represents a variety of viewpoints. The views implied or expressed in this handbook should not be interpreted as official opinions of Saint Andrew's School as a whole.

Copyright © 2003, 2006, 2007 by LuAnn Warner-Prokos, Tami Pleasanton, and Elizabeth Mulligan. All rights reserved. This book, in its entirety, may not be reproduced in any form without permission. Pages that involve a written activity may be reproduced only by the individual who purchases the book in order for that individual to repeat an activity. Publisher: Palm Tree Educational Press (10375 Rio Lindo, Delray Beach, Florida, 33446). This book was made possible with the support of Saint Andrew's School, Boca Raton, Florida.
ISBN 0-9777760-2-6
If you would like a copy, please visit our website: www.studyskillstoolkit.org

INTRODUCTION

Dear Student,

After examining an accumulation of over thirty years of educational research in learning styles and study skills, we present you with a compilation of meaningful advice, methods, activities, and reference materials. These specific learning strategies and reference materials will help you reach your academic goals. Learning is an art, requiring you to move beyond using rote skills. Our handbook is designed to lead you toward an understanding of your learning styles, preferences, and gifts (how you learn best and naturally) and gives recommendations how to utilize your personal academic strengths.

As with any art, mastery of learning is obtained through close attention to methods and materials as well as refinement of natural talents. We have included an appendix as a reference for additional information to assist you. This handbook is for you to pursue your highest level of academic mastery by using customized learning and organization structures.

As you work through various sections of this handbook, use a highlighter or writing utensil to mark critical information as it relates to your personal academic needs in mind, body, and spirit. You may want to record your thoughts, opinions, or questions as you go along. This process of marking your handbook will make it easy to review during your educational experience. Included in your book are additional response pages to the inventories. These can be used at later dates to see if your learning styles/preferences have changed over time.

We hope you approach this handbook with an open mind, ready to broaden your educational horizons. Give this experience a chance—you have nothing to lose!

Learning is fun!

To Teachers and Parents,

We, the editors, in no way want to assume that we are experts in the area of study skills. Although we have included a variety of instruments, they are not psycho-educational tools. They are meant only to help reveal strengths in student learning styles and profiles. In addition, we recognize that students' strengths change and grow as they mature; educational development is a process. We suggest that if a parent desires more extensive insight into his or her child's learning styles and competencies, the services of a licensed educational consultant may be productive. While this tool meets the needs of visual learners, it is our hope that teachers and students find additional methods to approach the advice offered in this text that would meet the needs of auditory and kinesthetic learners. For reference regarding operational definitions for terms used herein, please consult the glossary.

ABOUT THE EDITORS

LuAnn has over 18 years of experience in the history department in the Middle School at Saint Andrew's School, Boca Raton, Florida. Inspired by her students' needs, as well as her experiences at conferences and workshops on brain-based learning, learning styles, and innovative teaching methods, LuAnn initiated the writing of a workbook for Saint Andrew's students. She sought the help of Tami and Liz to create a well-rounded team. She has also taught a study skills course during the summer term, and she has presented at conferences, including an NAES conference, a Kagan seminar for an FCIS workshop, and a Summerbridge workshop. Desiring the latest pedagogy in study strategies for students, she attended a Quantum Learning conference in Chicago in the summer of 2003. In August 2005, she co-facilitated a Quantum Learning seminar at Saint Andrew's. LuAnn was named Teacher of the Year in May 2003. She has been subject coordinator in the Middle School and currently has an administrative role as Grade Leader for the 7th grade.

A 29-year teaching veteran with a Master's Degree in Classroom Instruction, **Tami**'s career as an elementary, middle, and high school mathematics teacher has been enhanced by nearly 15 years of administrative work as an Associate Head of School, Director of Admission, Dean of Students, Director of Community Service and Grade Leader. Awarded South Carolinas' Teacher of the Year in 1984, Tami returned to her home state of Florida in 1985 where she currently works as Associate Head of School and Director of Curriculum at Saint Joseph's Episcopal School. Tami regularly attends conferences and workshops on brain-based learning, learning styles, and innovative teaching methods. She has presented study skills workshops at national conferences, including NAES, and she co-facilitated a Quantum Learning seminar. Tami helped design our web site and has now begun work toward her doctoral degree in Education.

Liz has 21 years of experience in the field of education. Before relocating to South Florida, she taught history and was Associate Director of Admissions at two boarding schools in New England. She is a member of the American Society of Training and Development. Based upon information gleaned from various conferences and workshops on brain- based learning, learning styles, and innovative teaching methods, she was eager to participate in compiling the workbook with LuAnn and Tami. Liz has presented at various conferences, including an NAES conference, an FCIS conference, and a Kagan seminar. In her 13 years at Saint Andrew's, Liz has taught history in the Middle School and held various administrative positions. As part of this experience, she has acted as subject coordinator in the Middle School, Grade Leader, and she will begin her 9th year as Director of the Saint Andrew's Summer School (K – 12).

TABLE OF CONTENTS

I. How Do You Learn?..1
   • What Type of Learner Are You?......................................1
   • GASC Learning...6
   • Multiple Intelligence...10
   • My Learning Profile..15
   • Study Skills Checklist..23
   • Study Skills Survey...24

II. Goal Setting and Organization...27
   • Setting Goals..27
   • Organization—Daily Routines...28

III. Success In and Out of the Classroom..............................31
   • Eight Keys of Excellence...31
   • Success In the Classroom...32
   • SQ3R and Graphic Organizers...34
   • Summarizing...41

IV. Thinking Skills...42
   • Thinking..42
   • Memory..44
   • Concentration..48

V. Time and Stress Management...51

VI. Test and Exam Preparation...58
   • Preparing for Assessments...58
   • Taking Quizzes and Tests...59

VII. Appendix...61
   • Life Skills...61
   • Computers and Writing...64

VIII. Glossary..71

IX. Works Cited...74

X. Notes..75

XI. Additional Copies of Pages Containing Instruments (pp.1-24)....................81

XII. Parent/Teacher Addendum..101

Let's find out your learning preference. Are you a VISUAL, AUDITORY, or KINESTHETIC learner, or are you a COMBINATION? First, check the appropriate box for each question. Then, add up your checks going down the column, multiply the total by the number given, and add up the totals for each section. After you have answered the questions for all three sections, use the totals to graph your results.

LEARNING STYLES PROFILE
WHAT TYPE OF LEARNER ARE YOU?

VISUAL – AUDITORY – KINESTHETIC (V-A-K) ASSESSMENT
Mark the appropriate box for each question. Tally your score for each section.

VISUAL

	often	sometimes	seldom
◆ Are you neat and orderly?	☐	☐	☐
◆ Do you speak quickly?	☐	☐	☐
◆ Are you a good long-range planner and organizer?	☐	☐	☐
◆ Are you a good speller and can you actually see the words in your mind?	☐	☐	☐
◆ Do you remember what was seen rather than heard?	☐	☐	☐
◆ Do you memorize by visual association?	☐	☐	☐
◆ Do you have trouble remembering verbal instructions unless they are written down, and do you often ask people to repeat themselves?	☐	☐	☐
◆ Would you rather read than be read to?	☐	☐	☐
◆ Do you doodle during phone conversations/class/meetings?	☐	☐	☐
◆ Would you rather do a demonstration than make a speech?	☐	☐	☐
◆ Do you like art more than music?	☐	☐	☐
◆ Do you know what to say but can't think of the right words?	☐	☐	☐

subtotals = _____   _____   _____

x 2   x 1   x 0

totals = _____ + _____ + _____

(Note: additional pages to retake instrument can be found in the back.)   = _____

AUDITORY

	often	sometimes	seldom
◆ Do you speak to yourself while working?	☐	☐	☐
◆ Are you easily distracted by noise?	☐	☐	☐
◆ Do you move your lips/pronounce the words as you read?	☐	☐	☐
◆ Do you enjoy reading aloud and listening?	☐	☐	☐
◆ Can you repeat back and mimic tone, pitch, and timbre?	☐	☐	☐
◆ Do you find writing difficult, but are better at telling?	☐	☐	☐
◆ Do you speak in rhythmic patterns?	☐	☐	☐
◆ Do you think you're an eloquent speaker?	☐	☐	☐
◆ Do you like music more than art?	☐	☐	☐
◆ Do you learn by listening and remember what was discussed rather than seen?	☐	☐	☐
◆ Are you talkative, love discussion, and go into lengthy descriptions?	☐	☐	☐
◆ Can you spell better out loud than in writing?	☐	☐	☐

subtotals = _____   _____   _____

x 2   x 1   x 0

totals = _____ + _____ + _____

= _____

KINESTHETIC

	often	sometimes	seldom
◆ Do you speak loudly?	☐	☐	☐
◆ Do you touch people to get their attention?	☐	☐	☐
◆ Do you stand close when talking to someone?	☐	☐	☐
◆ Are you physically oriented and move a lot?	☐	☐	☐
◆ Do you learn by manipulating and doing?	☐	☐	☐
◆ Do you memorize by walking and seeing?	☐	☐	☐
◆ Do you use a finger as a pointer when reading?	☐	☐	☐
◆ Do you gesture a lot?	☐	☐	☐
◆ Do you have difficulty sitting still for long periods?	☐	☐	☐
◆ Do you make decisions based on your feelings?	☐	☐	☐
◆ Do you tap your pen, fingers or foot while listening?	☐	☐	☐
◆ Do you spend time playing sports and physical activities?	☐	☐	☐

subtotals = _____   _____   _____

x 2   x 1   x 0

totals = _____ + _____ + _____

= _____

Fill in the bar graph with your scores.

	V	A	K
24			
23			
22			
21			
20			
19			
18			
17			
16			
15			
14			
13			
12			
11			
10			
9			
8			
7			
6			
5			
4			
3			
2			
1			

Used by permission of Quantum Learning/SuperCamp, www.quantumlearning.com

WHAT DOES YOUR SCORE MEAN?

If you are a VISUAL LEARNER, you may want to:

- use symbols (stars, arrows) and create pictures in your notes.
- create your own mind-maps from notes (see page 34).
- try to get the "big picture" of a new chapter—scan the chapter, look at the pictures and graphs, read the questions at the end, look for main points given by the author.
- use charts and graphs.
- create note cards, columns, or rewrite notes or main points.
- envision the topic, or play out a movie in your mind of how you would act out the subject matter.

If you are an AUDITORY LEARNER, you may want to:

- listen to lectures and stories and repeat back the information.
- ask the teacher if you can repeat what was just said if you are unsure whether you understand what has been said.
- tape record yourself reading class notes and then listen to the recording before a quiz or test.
- talk it over to yourself aloud if you are struggling with a concept.
- make up a song to learn long strings of facts; use a well-known melody.
- listen to appropriate music when you study (soft tunes with no vocals; Baroque is appropriate).
- talk quietly to yourself (or to a stuffed animal or the wall) as you study.
- purchase books on tape for novels you are assigned.
- "listen" to the words as you read.
- try to act out an internal dialogue between you and the text as you read.

If you are a KINESTHETIC LEARNER, you may want to:

- "act out" your notes or move around as you study.
- sit on the floor or at a large table spreading everything out in front of you while studying at home.
- manipulate any small object such as a paper clip, bean bag, or crumpled piece of paper.
- tap your fingers to a beat on your leg or desk.
- apply what you are studying to a real life situation.
- highlight information meaningful to you.
- take notes in the margin, on paper, or on computer.
- redo notes from class on paper or computer.
- use a software program for graphic organizers, like *Inspiration.* ®

Used by permission of Quantum Learning/SuperCamp, www.quantumlearning.com

Reflections: Discuss what type of learner you are and list 3-4 strategies you might use this year.

_____
_____
_____
_____
_____
_____
_____
_____
_____
_____
_____
_____
_____

When you complete the above task, share your reflections with a peer.

Keep in mind that as you mature, your learning preferences and styles will MOST CERTAINLY change! Don't think this information is etched in stone—you may want to retest each year.

A huge part of how you understand and learn information comes from how you process it. You process information through any combination of organizing and conceptualizing material. Your processing preference may be dominantly Concrete/Sequential, Concrete/Global, Abstract/Sequential or Abstract/Global. Read each of the following brief descriptions to see which style you use to organize and conceptualize information for learning.

GASC LEARNING

Concrete/Sequential learners:

- are excellent organizers of daily routine.
- have neat desks with books carefully covered, clean and orderly.
- are usually those who remind the teacher about all the classroom chores.

If you feel you are Concrete/Sequential, you learn best from
- structured real experiences, such as field trips (where schedules are prearranged).
- working with models following step-by-step directions.
- observing and participating with the teacher in structured demonstration lessons.
- being involved in simulations that proceed from a set of rules, using step-by-step directions to complete a task.

Abstract/Sequential learners:

- often make sure their teacher specifies the due date of all assignments.
- want to know what to read, how to do it, and if it can be handwritten or if it must be typed-single spaced or double spaced.
- meet deadlines and often complete assignments well in advance.
- generally have very good grades, since abstract/sequential learning is the core of most testing.

If you feel you are Abstract/Sequential, you learn best from
- teaching strategies that involve a progression in reading, listening to verbal presentations (lectures, audio tapes), watching videotapes or films, and writing.
- playing mental games and gymnastics.
- using deductive reasoning.
- presenting a position through written or spoken word.
- making classifications.
- analyzing situations and problems.

Concrete/Global learners:

- are the ones who can put things together.
- can assemble a new kit in a classroom without using the directions.
- are the students who may have less than the best grades in a class, yet deep inside they are inventive and creative.
- use inductive reasoning and synthesizing.

If you feel you are Concrete/Global, you
- prefer learning with real things and the opportunity to explore all possibilities in searching for a solution.
- thrive best with optional assignments that involve real things, problem-solving simulations, unstructured field trips, learning through trial and error with real objects, committee work on real projects, and discovery learning.

Abstract/Global learners:

- are good readers of body language and the "vibes" in the class.
- are able to pick up nonverbal signals that aren't observed by the teacher or the rest of the group.
- are the natural synthesizers in a class discussion because their global organization allows them to bring the group's statements into a common focus and their abstract conceptualizing helps them put their ideas easily into words.

If you feel you are Abstract/Global, you

- profit from the opportunity to brainstorm in "thinking sessions" and during open-ended discussions.
- require "think time" to reflect before beginning a project or assignment.
- make intuitive leaps and synthesize for an "A ha!" experience.
- prefer optional and open-ended reading assignments and learning through discussion.

To learn more about the GASC research, contact Performance Learning Systems, Inc. at 1-800-757-3878.

Reflections: What is your processing/organizing preference?

_____
_____
_____
_____
_____
_____
_____
_____
_____
_____
_____
_____
_____
_____
_____

Activity
Here is another great way to gain information
about your unique learning preference(s).

1. Go to *Google* on your computer.
2. Type in the words "learning style preferences."
3. Select an instrument of your choice.
4. Complete the inventory according to their instructions.
5. Print out your score.
6. Below, summarize what you learned about your learning preference.

_____

_____

_____

_____

_____

_____

_____

_____

_____

Did you know that intelligence is measured in a variety of ways? Some people are "book smart," "socially smart," "math smart," and "environmentally smart," to name a few. Complete the following survey to see which category encompasses your strengths.

MULTIPLE INTELLIGENCE SURVEY–HOW ARE <u>YOU</u> SMART?

© Walter McKenzie, Surfaquarium Consulting

Part I

Complete each section by placing a "1" next to each statement you feel accurately describes you. If you do not identify with a statement, leave the space blank. Then total the column in each section.

Section 1:
_____ I enjoy categorizing things by common traits.
_____ Ecological issues are important to me.
_____ Hiking and camping are enjoyable activities.
_____ I enjoy working in a garden.
_____ I believe preserving our National Parks is important.
_____ Putting things first in hierarchies makes sense to me.
_____ Animals are important in my life.
_____ My home has a recycling system in place.
_____ I enjoy studying biology, botany, and/or zoology.
_____ I spend a great deal of time outdoors.

_____ = TOTAL for Section 1

Section 2:
_____ I easily pick up on patterns.
_____ I focus in on noise and sounds.
_____ Moving to a beat is easy for me.
_____ I've always been interested in playing an instrument.
_____ The cadence of poetry intrigues me.
_____ I remember things by putting them in a rhyme.
_____ Concentration is difficult while listening to a radio or television.
_____ I enjoy many kinds of music.
_____ Musicals are more interesting than dramatic plays.
_____ Remembering song lyrics is easy for me.

_____ = TOTAL for Section 2

Section 3:

_____ I keep my things neat and orderly.

_____ Step-by-step directions are a big help.

_____ Solving problems comes easily to me.

_____ I get easily frustrated with disorganized people.

_____ I can complete calculations quickly in my head.

_____ Puzzles requiring reasoning are fun.

_____ I can't begin an assignment until all my questions are answered.

_____ Structures help me be successful.

_____ I find working on a computer spreadsheet or database rewarding.

_____ Things have to make sense to me or I am dissatisfied.

_____ = TOTAL for Section 3

Section 4:

_____ It is important to see my role in the "big picture" of things.

_____ I enjoy discussing questions about life.

_____ Religion is important to me.

_____ I enjoy viewing art masterpieces.

_____ Relaxation and meditation exercises are rewarding.

_____ I like visiting breathtaking sites in nature.

_____ I enjoy reading ancient and modern philosophers.

_____ Learning new things is easier when I understand their value.

_____ I wonder if there are other forms of intelligent life in the universe.

_____ Studying history and ancient culture helps give me perspective.

_____ = TOTAL for Section 4

Section 5:

_____ I learn best interacting with others.

_____ The more the merrier!

_____ Study groups are very productive for me.

_____ I enjoy chat rooms.

_____ Participating in politics is important.

_____ Television and radio talk shows are enjoyable.

_____ I am a "team player."

_____ I dislike working alone.

_____ Clubs and extracurricular activities are fun.

_____ I pay attention to social issues and causes.   _____ = TOTAL for Section 5

Section 6:

____ I enjoy making things with my hands.

____ Sitting still for long periods of time is difficult for me.

____ I enjoy outdoor games and sports.

____ I value non-verbal communication, such as sign language.

____ A fit body is important for a fit mind.

____ Arts and crafts are enjoyable pastimes.

____ Expression through dance is beautiful.

____ I like working with tools.

____ I live an active lifestyle.

____ I learn by doing.

____ = TOTAL for Section 6

Section 7:

____ I enjoy reading all kinds of materials.

____ Taking notes helps me remember and understand.

____ I faithfully contact friends through letters and/or e-mail.

____ It is easy for me to explain my ideas to others.

____ I keep a journal.

____ Word puzzles like crosswords and jumbles are fun.

____ I write for pleasure.

____ I enjoy playing with words like puns, anagrams, and spoonerisms.

____ Foreign languages interest me.

____ Debates and public speaking are activities in which I like to participate.

____ = TOTAL for Section 7

Section 8:

____ I am keenly aware of my moral beliefs.

____ I learn best when I have an emotional attachment to the subject.

____ Fairness is important to me.

____ My attitude effects how I learn.

____ Social justice issues concern me.

____ Working alone can be just as productive as working in a group.

____ I need to know why I should do something before I agree to do it.

____ When I believe in something I will give 100% effort to it.

____ I like to be involved in causes that help others.

____ I am willing to protest or sign a petition to right a wrong.

____ = TOTAL for Section 8

Section 9:
____ I can imagine ideas in my mind.
____ Rearranging a room is fun for me.
____ I enjoy creating art using varied media.
____ I remember well using graphic organizers.
____ Performance art can be very gratifying.
____ Spreadsheets are great for making charts, graphs, and tables.
____ Three dimensional puzzles bring me much enjoyment.
____ Music videos are very stimulating.
____ I can recall things in mental pictures.
____ I am good at reading maps and blueprints.

____ = TOTAL for Section 9

Part II

Using this chart, record your totals from each section and multiply each total by 10.

Section	Total	Multiply	Score
1		x10	
2		x10	
3		x10	
4		x10	
5		x10	
6		x10	
7		x10	
8		x10	
9		x10	

Part III

Plot your scores on the bar graph provided.

100									
90									
80									
70									
60									
50									
40									
30									
20									
10									
0	Sec 1	Sec 2	Sec 3	Sec 4	Sec 5	Sec 6	Sec 7	Sec 8	Sec 9

Part IV

Find your strength below and then **look up it's definition** in the **glossary**.

Key:

Section 1 – This reflects your NATURALIST strength.
Section 2 – This suggests your MUSICAL strength.
Section 3 – This indicates your LOGICAL strength.
Section 4 – This illustrates your EXISTENTIAL strength.
Section 5 – This shows your INTERPERSONAL strength.
Section 6 – This tells your KINESTHETIC strength.
Section 7 – This indicates your VERBAL strength.
Section 8 – This reflects your INTRAPERSONAL strength.
Section 9 – This suggests your VISUAL strength.

REMEMBER:
☺ Everyone possesses, to some degree, all the intelligences!
☺ You can strengthen an intelligence!
☺ This survey is meant as a snapshot in time – it can and will change!
☺ Knowing your Multiple Intelligence strengths are meant to empower, not label!

Permission to reprint from © Walter McKenzie, Surfaquarium Consulting, http://surfaquarium.com/mi.htm), 1999.

Your learning profile will provide insights into how you prefer to study. Complete the profile below to determine your learning preferences. Check each statement that you <u>strongly believe</u> is true for you. Leave the <u>others blank</u>. Then add up the number of checks in each section.

MY LEARNING PROFILE

Sound
Some people like Bach, some people like boom.
Some people have to study where it's silent as a tomb.
Do you need noise? Do you need quiet?
How will you know? You'll know if you try it.

- ☐ When I study I prefer quiet!
- ☐ Traffic, music, the TV, airplanes, and talking keep me from concentrating.
- ☐ People or other students who move, squirm, erase papers, tap with their feet, or pencil, or ruler really bother me when I'm studying or reading.
- ☐ Sometimes I have to cover my ears with my hands so that I can concentrate on what I am studying.

Number of checks:____ (1A)

- ☐ When I study I prefer to do it with music.
- ☐ I just can't concentrate when the room is absolutely quiet.
- ☐ I feel comfortable when the TV or stereo is on when I study.
- ☐ When I do my homework or read, I like to be in a place where other people are talking and working.

Number of checks:____ (1B)

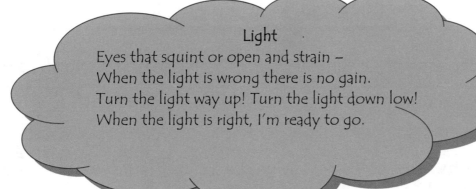

Light

Eyes that squint or open and strain –
When the light is wrong there is no gain.
Turn the light way up! Turn the light down low!
When the light is right, I'm ready to go.

☐ When I study I put on all the lights.
☐ I like to read or do homework outdoors.
☐ I often get sleepy or can't concentrate unless I have on bright lights.
☐ I always move to the windows or under large banks of light when I study.

Number of checks:_____ (2A)

☐ I prefer to read in low or very dim light.
☐ I like to do homework with most of the lights off.
☐ I like to use just one small lamp when I do my homework.
☐ I can read under tables and in dark corners.

Number of checks:_____(2B)

Temperature

The wrong degree of heat inside
Can make those facts just slip and slide.
Some like it warm, some like it cool—
The temp in the room is a learning tool.

☐ I prefer the warmer weather school months.
☐ I study best in a warm room.
☐ I usually wear sweaters or extra clothes indoors.
☐ I often feel too cold and prefer the heat on when I do homework.

Number of checks:_____ (3A)

☐ I prefer the cooler weather school months.
☐ I prefer it to be cool when I study.
☐ I don't wear sweaters and extra clothes indoors; they make me feel too warm.
☐ I often feel too warm, and I like the heat off when I do homework.

Number of checks:_____ (3B)

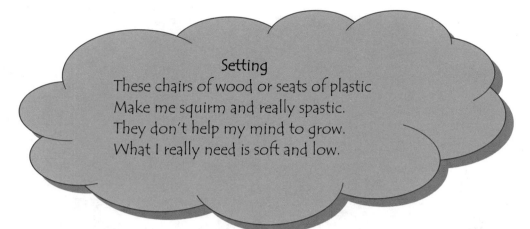

Setting
These chairs of wood or seats of plastic
Make me squirm and really spastic.
They don't help my mind to grow.
What I really need is soft and low.

☐ I prefer to do homework at a table or desk.
☐ I get sleepy or lazy if I try to read on a bed or couch.
☐ I like to sit up straight when I study or write.
☐ I just can't concentrate if I lie down or stretch out when I study.

Number of checks:____ (4A)

☐ I like to sit on a soft chair or couch when I study.
☐ I can't concentrate too well when I sit at a desk or table.
☐ I often read on the floor.
☐ Sometimes I work on my bed or stretched out on a couch.

Number of checks:____ (4B)

Self
Learning by myself is what suits me,
Like a strong proud eagle flying free.
No one to hurry, no one to race—
Just going along at my own pace.

☐ I really like to work by myself.
☐ I usually don't prefer to work in groups.
☐ I do work best by myself!
☐ Don't send someone to help me.

Number of checks:____ (5A)

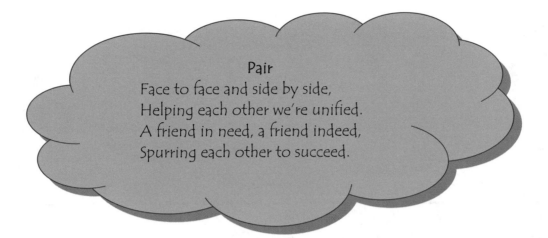

Pair
Face to face and side by side,
Helping each other we're unified.
A friend in need, a friend indeed,
Spurring each other to succeed.

☐ I prefer to study with one person.
☐ I get more done when I have a partner.
☐ I learn more if I can ask questions of
a friend and we talk about it.
☐ I like to describe what I'm learning to a partner.

Number of checks:_____ (5B)

Team
Studying with others in a team or loop,
All tasks are a snap in a working group.
We all chip in and even have fun,
But we keep going 'til the job is done.

☐ It's fun to work on a project with friends.
☐ I prefer to work with a team or committee.
☐ We all help each other in a group.
☐ I need several people to talk about things so I understand what to learn.

Number of checks:_____ (5C)

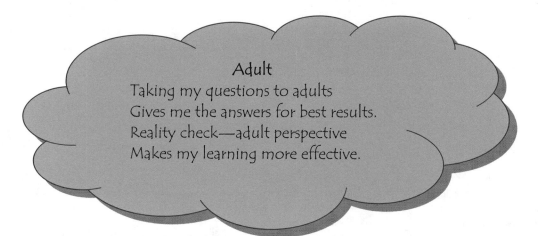

Adult
Taking my questions to adults
Gives me the answers for best results.
Reality check—adult perspective
Makes my learning more effective.

- ☐ I need the teacher to show me how to do things.
- ☐ I like it when the teacher checks my work.
- ☐ I like to work with the teacher, my parents, or an adult when I'm alone with one of them.
- ☐ I prefer to discuss things with an adult.

Number of checks:_____ (5D)

Varied
Some people like a change of scene,
Some people need the same routine
For learning things the same old way.
While others change from day to day.

- ☐ Sometimes I like to work alone or with a friend or the teacher.
- ☐ I like to work with different people.
- ☐ I like to do my assignments in different ways, alone and with others.
- ☐ When we work in groups I like different ways of doing things.

Number of checks:_____ (5E)

Senses
Do you SEE what I mean?
Do you HEAR what I say?
Are you getting in TOUCH?
Are you MOVING my way?
What's your preference?
How do you learn?
You can learn it all
It is your turn.

Seeing pictures
☐ I can really learn it if I see it on TV or in a movie.
☐ I like computer programs with pictures.
☐ I like to read books with diagrams and pictures.
☐ I like to sketch, underline, and use colors or my own symbols when I take notes.
Number of checks:____ (6A)

Seeing words
☐ I learn best if I read about it.
☐ I like computer programs with lots of words.
☐ I prefer assignments with clear directions in words I understand.
☐ I like word games like Scrabble™.
Number of checks:____(6B)

Listening
☐ I learn best when I hear the teacher explain something.
☐ I can learn by listening to audio tape.
☐ I remember things best when I talk about them with someone.
☐ I can remember things when someone reads them to me.
Number of checks:____(6C)

Touching
☐ I learn best with puzzles and games.
☐ I like to make and build things.
☐ I really enjoy working with my hands.
☐ I prefer learning material that I can touch and move.
Number of checks:____(6D)

Doing/moving
☐ I like homework assignments that ask me to do things away from school.
☐ I like charades, games, and projects where I do things and have to move.
☐ I prefer learning something by acting, role-playing, interviewing, reporting, by getting all of me involved.
☐ Field trips help me to understand what I'm learning in school.
Number of checks:____(6E)

Time of day
In the morning, my blood doesn't flow,
My brain is slow, can't get up and go.
I rise with the sun, I'll rest later
'Cause in the evening I'm a couch potato.

Morning:
- ☐ I remember things better in early classes of the day.
- ☐ Usually I like to get up between 6 a.m. and 8 a.m.
- ☐ I wish I could take classes beginning no later than 8 a.m.
- ☐ I would like to begin school early and end before 2 o'clock.

Number of checks:____ (7A)

Mid-day:
- ☐ Usually I like to get up between 8 a.m. and 10 a.m.
- ☐ I start to come alive after 10 a.m.
- ☐ I wish I could study the most difficult subjects just before lunch.
- ☐ I like to work with teachers or other students in the late morning.

Number of checks:____ (7B)

Afternoon:
- ☐ I wish school would begin after lunch.
- ☐ I like to do my homework right after I get home from school.
- ☐ I'm most alert toward the end of the school day.
- ☐ I wish I could take my most difficult classes between 1 p.m. and 4 p.m.

Number of checks:____ (7C)

Evening:
- ☐ I like to stay up late to do my homework.
- ☐ I feel wide awake when I'm supposed to go to sleep.
- ☐ I wish school would start at night.
- ☐ I would like to work on school assignments with teachers or other students after 8 p.m.

Number of checks:____ (7D)

Fill in the number of responses for each section.
4 checks = strong preference, 3 checks = preference

sound:
(1A) Quiet _____
(1B) Sound _____

lights:
(2A) Bright _____
(2B) Dim/soft _____

temperature:
(3A) Warm _____
(3B) Cool _____

setting:
(4A) Formal _____
(4B) Informal _____

learning groups:
(5A) Self _____   (5B) Pair _____   (5C) Team _____
(5D) Adult _____   (5E) Varied _____

senses:
(6A) Seeing Pictures _____
(6B) Seeing Words _____
(6C) Listening _____
(6D) Touching _____
(6E) Doing/Moving _____

time of day:
(7A) Morning _____
(7B) Mid-Day _____
(7C) Afternoon _____
(7D) Evening _____

Used by permission of Quantum Learning/SuperCamp, www.quantumlearning.com

Reflections: How will you use this
information about yourself to study?

_____
_____
_____
_____
_____
_____
_____
_____
_____
_____
_____
_____
_____
_____

Activity – AN ONLINE INVENTORY
STUDY SKILLS CHECKLIST:

1. Go to the following website: http://www.ucc.vt.edu
   The purpose of this inventory is to discover information about your own study habits and attitudes.

2. Scroll down the list and click on "Study Skills Self-Help Info." See list.

3. At the end of the page, click "Study Skills Inventory" icon. This will send you to pages on the website for help with scheduling, concentration, listening and note-taking, reading, exams, and writing skills. If you answered one "yes" or all "no"s in any of the categories you are probably proficient enough in that area. You may still want to read through the suggestions in areas that interest you.

4. <u>Write</u> a 5-7 sentence paragraph summarizing your strengths and weaknesses and some strategies to improve.

5. For more activities on this site, click on any of the five categories under "Online Study Skills Workshops."

_____
_____
_____
_____
_____
_____
_____
_____
_____
_____
_____
_____
_____
_____
_____

For another site with inventories and more information on brain-based learning: www.gigglepotz.com/mistudent.htm
Scroll and click on "Student Questionaire." Take the test and score results.

For information on your learning style after you have taken one or both of the assessments, see pages 4 and 5 of this handbook.

24

Let's see how you would evaluate yourself on your study skills before we go any further.

STUDY SKILLS SURVEY

Read the following statements to assess how competent you feel at this point in your educational career with regards to study skills. Check those that apply to you and tally your marks. A total of 10 would mean you feel you have mastered that skill; a 5 would mean you are somewhat competent, and a 1 would mean you lack that skill. BE HONEST WITH YOURSELF!! Honest self-assessment is a vital part of learning.

1. ☐ I am able to set realistic academic and personal goals.
2. ☐ I understand how I learn best.
3. ☐ I am able to manage my time to meet school, activity, and relaxation needs.
4. ☐ As I read my textbooks, I am able to learn what is essential for the class.
5. ☐ I am able to stay alert and focused during class.
6. ☐ I take lecture notes that are complete, clear, and useful.
7. ☐ I am able to listen effectively to get the most out of class discussions.
8. ☐ I use a variety of strategies to remember information.
9. ☐ I know what type of study space I need in order to do my work well.
10. ☐ I can differentiate between essential and non-essential information in class discussions.
11. ☐ I can differentiate between essential and non-essential information in my textbook readings.
12. ☐ I am able to motivate myself to study.
13. ☐ I am able to stay on top of my course work.
14. ☐ I am good at testing myself to see if I really understand information.
15. ☐ I am able to study course materials so that I understand and can retain information for exams.
16. ☐ I study effectively for exams.
17. ☐ I take exams in an efficient and systematic manner ("Study Skills Survey" 1).

Activity

Use the lines below and on the next page to discuss what areas you would like to learn about in order to improve your academic success during the school year. You may also want to reflect on what you have learned about yourself as a whole after taking one or more of these inventories.

_____

_____

_____

Notes: _____

_____

_____

_____

_____

_____

_____

_____

_____

_____

_____

_____

_____

_____

_____

_____

_____

_____

_____

_____

_____

_____

_____

_____

_____

_____

_____

_____

_____

_____

_____

_____

_____

_____

_____

_____

_____

_____

_____

_____

_____

_____

_____

_____

_____

_____

_____

_____

_____

You probably know some athlete, musician, or writer whom you admire because he or she is successful. Obviously, these people have natural gifts, but they also work hard. You probably know about setting goals and organizing your time, but there is always room for improvement. Everyone should learn about setting realistic goals, managing time wisely, completing assignments on time, and managing stress in life.

SETTING GOALS

- Set one or two basic goals for the marking period/semester/year (for example, strive to earn a higher grade in a course that is difficult for you or plan to practice your musical instrument for 1-2 hours every weekend).
- Write out your goals and display them prominently.
  - Write your goals in your daily academic planner so you see them every day.
- Make your goals attainable.
  - Improve yourself in small steps.
  - Be flexible. You may have a setback or two, but don't give up; realistic goals can be reached.
  - Give yourself time to achieve your goals – seek gradual improvement.
  - Break big goals into smaller ones (for example, work on a project twenty minutes instead of working for three hours straight).
- Revise your goals when necessary.
  - Circumstances change – don't beat yourself up.
  - If you do not reach a goal in the way you thought you should, try, try again!!

Reflections: Write two short-term goals.
1. _____
_____
2. _____
Write two long-term goals.
1. _____
_____
2. _____

Praise yourself at the end of each day for goals met. Think of at least two ways your day was good. Think about happy things!!!

DAILY ROUTINE

- Be ready!
    - *Feed your brain!
        - –The brain is only 2% of the body's adult weight, but it consumes about 20% of the body's energy.
        - –Feed it with brain foods, such as eggs, leafy green vegetables, wheat germ, chicken, fruits, and fish. Start each day with a nutritious breakfast.
        - –Eat balanced meals.
    - *Drink plenty of water.
        - –Without it, you become restless, headachy, and unfocused.
        - –The body can best absorb water when you drink in small amounts.
        - –Bring a water bottle to school and sip water throughout the day.

- Do some type of exercise every day!
    - *Exercise can energize you.
    - *Exercise helps you sleep better at night.
    - *Exercise helps fight sadness/depression.
- Get adequate sleep each night!
    - *DO: –get up and go to bed at approximately the same time every day.
        - –develop sleep rituals.
        - –make sure your bedroom is quiet and comfortable.
        - –read something you like or do some journaling before bedtime.
    - *DON'T: exercise immediately before bedtime.
    - *Before bedtime:
        - –eliminate caffeine.
        - –eat a healthy snack.
        - –take a hot bath/shower 90 minutes before bedtime.
- Preview your daily schedule!
    - *With a rotating/block schedule, know what class you have first.
    - *Pack your backpack accordingly.
- Improve your mind.
    - *Read part of the newspaper, magazine, or a book each day.
    - *Visualize success.

Eat a healthy breakfast each day. Your brain and muscles need the energy boost nutritious foods offer. Too much sugar or caffeine can give you energy that lasts only for a while, and then leaves you tired. Soft drinks, fruit juices, teas, and coffee do not hydrate the brain as effectively as water.

Reflections: Referring back to pages 27-28, <u>list</u> five points you believe are important. <u>Draw</u> a picture to represent each of the points.

1. _____

2. _____

3. _____

4. _____

5. _____

Before each quiz/test, you should visualize taking it and doing well.
Write a phrase or two that you might tell yourself.

_____
_____
_____
_____
_____
_____
_____
_____

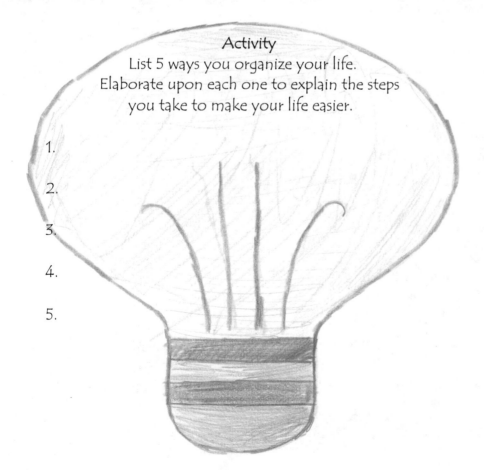

Activity
List 5 ways you organize your life.
Elaborate upon each one to explain the steps
you take to make your life easier.

1.

2.

3.

4.

5.

BE ORGANIZED

*Organize your backpack.
 -no loose papers, non-school materials, or junk
 -leave heavy texts out; carry them to and from home and school

*Organize your locker.
 -use shelves
 -have a pouch for extra pens, pencils, and highlighters
 -keep extra lined paper handy
 -no loose papers

*Organize your notebooks.
 -keep track of quizzes and tests
 -use dividers to keep notes separate from homework assignments
 -have extra lined paper at the back
 -file all loose papers into appropriate sections
 -organize once a week

*Use your academic planner.
 -write clearly
 -transfer homework handout assignments, or staple homework assignment
   sheets to planner
 -schedule assignments - write all for the week, if given
 -projects, papers, books – plan out a weekly schedule to complete
 -post sports game times and dates
 -write extra-curricular activities
 -have the phone number of a homework pal available
 -check off assignments as they are completed

*Keep your workspace at home neat.
 -keep clutter-free
 -have extra supplies on hand
 -keep a dictionary and thesaurus nearby
 -use a clock – be sure to take breaks every 20-30 minutes

The following principles help everyone in the classroom. They guide behavior, help establish a trusting and supportive environment, and create an atmosphere where everyone is valued and respected. According to the Greeks, everything you do — conversations and interactions with strangers, family, and friends — reveals your true character. Honesty, persistence, and dependability are admirable qualities that will take you far.

EIGHT KEYS OF EXCELLENCE

INTEGRITY
Conduct yourself with authenticity, sincerity, and wholeness. Your values and behavior are aligned.

FAILURE LEADS TO SUCCESS
Understand that failures simply provide you with the information you need to succeed. There are no failures, only outcomes and feedback. Each event can be useful if you know how to find the gift.

SPEAK WITH GOOD PURPOSE
Speak in a positive sense and be responsible for honest and direct communication. Avoid gossip and harmful communication.

THIS IS IT
Focus your attention on the present moment and make the most of it. Give each task your best effort.

COMMITMENT
Follow through on promises and obligations; live your vision. Make whatever changes it takes to get the job done.

OWNERSHIP
Take responsibility and be accountable for your actions.

FLEXIBILITY
Be open to change or a new approach when it helps you attain the outcome you desire.

BALANCE
Keep your mind, body, and spirit in alignment. Spend time developing and maintaining these three areas.

For more information, see Quantum Teaching by Bobbi DePorter, et al.
Used by permission of Quantum Learning/SuperCamp, www.quantumlearning.com

REFOCUS AT THE BEGINNING OF EACH CLASS

*Stretch before sitting down.

*Stretch arms and legs during class if you find you are losing focus.

*Hand in any missing work.

*Take out what you will need for that class: planner, writing utensils, text, notebook, etc.

*Remember "This Is It" – focus on the class, NOT upon what is going on with friends outside of class.

TAKING EFFECTIVE NOTES

*Note-taking helps you pay attention, understand better, and remember more.

*Always label notes: date, topic, and page number.

*Copy everything the teacher puts on the board.

*Ask for clarification if you become confused.

*Keep up with the pace of any discussion.

*Listen for important verbal clues AND take notes:

    "This is important."

    "First…Second…Third…"

    "Don't forget this."

    "This will be on the test."

*Use a pen that won't smudge.

*Use shortcuts or abbreviations for long words or passages.

*Leave 1/3 page free (either right or left side) to write your thoughts or questions.

*Leave spaces between notes so you can add more later.

REVIEW YOUR NOTES

*Always review class notes each day – you may want to read out loud or explain to someone. Write a funny song with your notes, tell yourself a story, create flashcards or a matching game.

*Write questions you may have in the margins of your notes.

*Use a highlighter to mark important parts.

*Rewrite notes if they are sloppy.

*Rewrite notes in a different way using graphic organizers (see pages 34-38) or software programs like *Inspiration*.® (www.inspiration.com/beta.html)

*Keep a "Learning Log" or journal.

    -This is especially helpful for a subject that is hard for you.

    -Write down thoughts, feelings, reactions, and questions about what you are studying.

    -You can write your first thoughts or the importance of an event or application.

    -You may want to write about a topic that confuses you or interests you, and then show it to your teacher before or after class.

REFRESH BETWEEN CLASSES

*Get a drink of water.
*Use the restroom.
*Move around.
*Mingle with friends!

READING ASSIGNMENTS FOR MEANING

*You are reading for understanding with textbooks AND when conducting research.
*Become an "active" reader rather than a "passive" one - ask yourself questions as you read.
*Follow the SQ3R method (Survey, Question, Read, Recite/Write, Review; see page 34). Read to answer the "who, what, how, why, where, when" questions. Use outlining, mind-mapping, or other graphic organizers (see pages 34-38).
*First preview what you are to read - look at all headings, illustrations, questions, and bold-type words.
*Read assignment carefully - look for main ideas, supporting details/facts, vocabulary words; REREAD difficult parts.
*Highlight the information.
*Review what you have read - take outline notes or use a graphic organizer (see pages 34-38), make flash cards, summarize in a paragraph, or explain to someone; use headings/sub-headings for YOUR headings; leave spaces to add more.

HIGHLIGHTING

*Read a section or entire assignment first.
*In each paragraph:
  -highlight topic sentence, if there is one.
  -highlight vocabulary words and definitions.
*Do not highlight an entire sentence, just main phrase/words.
*Do not highlight an entire paragraph.

Reading for fun and leisure can help you improve reading for school!

SQ3R

This method should be used whenever you read a text or other assigned material. Use one of the following graphic organizers when you write your notes.

SURVEY assignment: Look through all pages, including pictures, graphs, and questions.

QUESTION: Ask yourself questions, read the author's questions, write bold print into questions, and turn headings into questions.

READ carefully: Underline/highlight answers to the questions you created.

RECITE/WRITE what you have learned: Try to answer the "who, what, why..." questions. This should be done as soon as possible after reading the assignment.

REVIEW or summarize what you have read. Review previous work each night until the next quiz or test.

Mind-Mapping/Webbing:

You can make up your own mind-map or use software programs such as *Inspiration*® (see example below). This software also includes picture graphics to enhance your mind-maps.

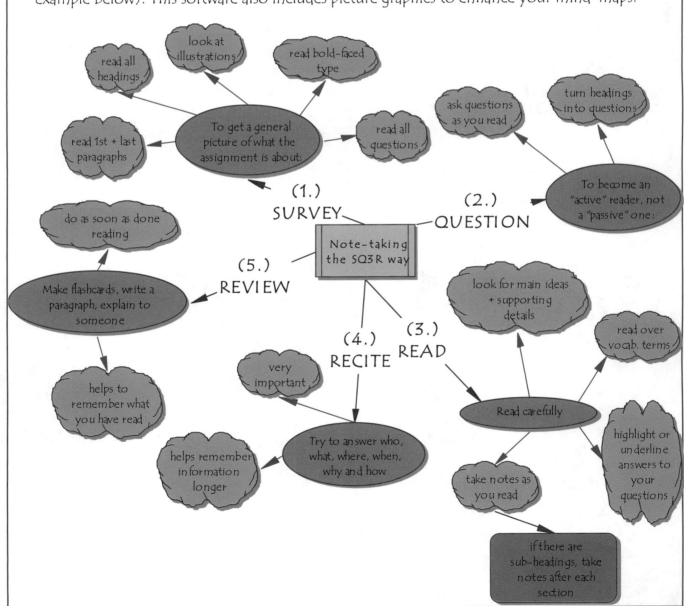

Outline

I. Main topic
    A. Supporting detail/fact
    B. Supporting detail/fact
        1. Sub-detail
         a)
           i)
           ii)
        2. Sub detail
II. Main topic
    A. Supporting detail/fact
        1. Sub-detail
        2. Sub-detail
        3. Sub-detail

Note: You can also create your own system, using symbols for bullet points:
*, →, ●, ▶, ≈, –, ↓, =, etc...

Continue: III, IV, V, VI, VII, VIII, IX, X, XI, XII….XX, etc.

I. Nutrients and Digestion
    A. Why do you eat?
        1. Energy Needs
         a) Nutrients – substances in foods that provide energy and materials for cell development, growth, and repair
    B. Classes of Nutrients
        1. Proteins – needed for replacement and repair of body cells and for growth – large molecules that contain carbon, hydrogen, oxygen, nitrogen, and sometimes sulfur
         a) amino acids
        2. Carbohydrates – main sources of energy for your body – made of carbon, hydrogen, and oxygen atoms
         a) simple carbohydrates
           i) fruits
           ii) milk
         b) complex carbohydrates
           i) potatoes
           ii) pasta
        3. Fats – also called lipids – provide energy, help your body absorb vitamins, and cushion your internal organs
         a) unsaturated
           i) vegetable oils (liquid at room temperature)
         b) saturated
           i) found in meats (solid at room temperature)
        4. Vitamins – used for regulating body functions and preventing some diseases
         a) water-soluble
         b) fat-soluble

Table Organizers

Using a chart for organizing information about a novel
Title: <u>Of Mice and Men</u>
Author: John Steinbeck
Main Characters:
<u>George Milton</u> – A farmhand who accepts day labor and who has assumed the responsibility of taking care of his simple-minded friend, Lennie.
<u>Lennie Small</u> – A large, retarded man who has the mind of a child and who loves to pet soft, pretty things.
<u>Slim</u> – A sympathetic farmhand who understands and consoles George when Lennie is killed.
<u>Candy</u> – An old, crippled farmhand who has saved some money and wants to be a part of George and Lennie's plan to buy a place of their own.
<u>Crooks</u> – A black farmhand who keeps to himself and is estranged from the white workers.
<u>Carlson</u> – The farmhand responsible for killing the old, blind dog that belonged to Candy.
<u>Curley</u> – A small, cocky, arrogant man who is the son of the boss.
<u>Curley's Wife</u> – The woman is given no name; she tries to make friends with Lennie.

Title:	<u>Of Mice and Men</u>
Author:	John Steinbeck
Main Characters: <u>George Milton</u>	<u>George Milton</u> – A farmhand who accepts day labor and who has assumed the responsibility of taking care of his simple-minded friend, Lennie.
<u>Lennie Small</u>	<u>Lennie Small</u> – A large, retarded man who has the mind of a child and who loves to pet soft, pretty things.
<u>Slim</u>	<u>Slim</u> – A sympathetic farmhand who understands and consoles George when Lennie is killed.
<u>Candy</u>	<u>Candy</u> – An old, crippled farmhand who has saved some money and wants to be a part of George and Lennie's plan to buy a place of their own.
<u>Crooks</u>	<u>Crooks</u> – A black farmhand who keeps to himself and is aloof from the white workers.
<u>Carlson</u>	<u>Carlson</u> – The farmhand responsible for killing the old, blind dog that belonged to Candy.
<u>Curley</u>	<u>Curley</u> – A small, cocky, arrogant man who is the son of the boss.
<u>Curley's Wife</u>	<u>Curley's Wife</u> – The woman is given no name; she tries to make friends with Lennie.

Note: There are many other categories to include, such as theme, setting, conflict, etc.
Another great table organizer is the Cornell Note-taking System. See page 40 for an activity and information.

Venn Diagram
Title: Federal System

National Government
(Delegated Powers)
Coin money and regulate its value
Establish postal system
Regulate interstate and foreign commerce
Declare war
Make treaties with foreign nations
Create and maintain armed forces
Regulate naturalization of aliens
Protect federal property throughout country

National and State Government
(Concurrent Powers)
Levy and collect taxes
Borrow money
Set up courts

State Governments
(Reserved Powers)
Provide system of education
Regulate marriage and divorce
Establish voting qualifications (but states may not deny suffrage on basis of race, color, or sex, or withhold voting rights from 18-year-old citizens)
Provide local governments
Regulate commerce within boundaries of state (intrastate)
Build intrastate roads and other public works

Federal System

National Government
(Delegated Powers)
-Coin money and regulate its value
-Establish postal system
-Regulate interstate and foreign commerce
-Declare war
-Make treaties with foreign nations
-Create and maintain armed forces
-Regulate naturalization of aliens
-Protect federal property throughout country

National and State Governments
(Concurrent Powers)
-Levy and collect taxes
-Borrow money
-Set up courts

State Governments
(Reserved Powers)
-Provide system of education
-Regulate marriage and divorce
-Establish voting qualifications (but states may not deny suffrage on basis of race, color, or sex, or withhold voting rights from 18-year-old citizens)
-Provide local governments
-Regulate commerce within boundaries of state (intrastate)
-Build intrastate roads and other public works

Note: You may want to use abbreviations or symbols.

Cause and Effect

<u>Need for Soil Conservation</u>

Causes	*Effects*
Development	Erosion
Mining	Nutrient depletion
Agriculture	Crop rotation
	Desertification
	Land reclamation

Causes:

1. Development   2. Mining   3. Agriculture

Need for Soil Conservation

Effects:

| 1. Erosion | 2. Nutrient depletion | 3. Crop rotation |
| 4. Desertification | 5. Land reclamation | |

KWL Chart

K	W	L
"What do I <u>Know</u>?"	"What do I need/<u>Want</u> to know?"	"What have I <u>Learned</u>?"
-Write what you already know about the topic.	-Pause as you read. -With each paragraph, look for main ideas, details, definitions, and then highlight information. -Write questions you have, definitions, and important information to remember.	-Take notes on what you have learned.

(Sebranek et al. 321)

Activity
Select a topic and create your own mind-map.

Activity
Cornell Note-taking System

FIRST: On notebook paper, draw an upside down "T" as shown on this page. This side is used for lecture or text notes. Write headings, sub-headings, and bullet points (ideas written in phrases). Use abbreviations in notes whenever possible. Then, summarize your words in the box at the bottom of the page.

Example:

A. HEADING:

1.   SUB-HEADING:
   • fact or idea written in phrase format, not sentences
   • fact or idea written in phrase format
   • fact or idea written in phrase format
      - example or supporting detail

2.   SUB-HEADING
   • fact or idea written in phrase format, not sentences
   • fact or idea written in phrase format
   • fact or idea written in phrase format

Activity: Practice this method for one of your subjects. Read a section and follow the instructions on this page.

SECOND: After lecture or for review of your notes, write key words or phrases in your own words that will be a cue for notes you have written to the right. These cues can be single words (vocabulary), questions, names, formulas, etc.

THIRD: Cover the notes to the right and read your cues to the left. Review until you can recite the fact or idea that correlates (connects) with the cue.

SUMMARIZE: Use this section to summarize the main ideas from the lecture or your text notes. Use complete sentences.

For more information, see the following websites:
1)   www.clt.cornell.edu/campus/learn/LSC Resources/cornellsystem.pdf
2)   www.ucc.vt.edu/stdysk/cornell.html
3)   www.dartmouth.edu/~acskills/docs/cornell_note_taking.doc

Summarizing is an essential skill. By summarizing you can determine if you understand what you have read or heard. As you summarize, you are forced to accurately tell or write the presented key ideas in your own words. Summarizing leads to deeper understanding and better recall of the lessons. While the process of summarizing is somewhat automatic to most of you, there are strategies for this process.

SUMMARIZING
FICTION, NONFICTION, TEXTS

Rule-Based Summarizing Strategy Model
1. Delete unimportant material that is unnecessary to your understanding.
2. Delete repeated information.
3. Substitute a list of things with a word that describes the specific terms (For example, use "tools" for "flat head screw driver," "hammer," or "scroll saw").
4. Find a topic sentence, or invent one if it is missing (Marzano et al. 57).

Guidelines for Writing a Summary
1. Skim the assigned reading to develop a "big picture" of the material.
2. Read the section carefully while focusing on key terms and topics (try SQ3R, page 34).
3. Without looking at the section, make a list of the main ideas.
4. Review the selection to clearly understand the information as you prepare to write.
5. Write a summary of the major ideas <u>using your own words</u>. You may use a few words from the reading that cannot be changed. These words should be in quotation marks. DO NOT just change a few words with a thesaurus.
   - Write a topic sentence containing the main idea of the section.
   - Write about the essential information: names, dates, times, places and similar facts, descriptions and examples. Avoid using adjectives and pronouns.
6. Check your summary to ensure you have written correct information in a concise manner. Review these questions as you check your summary:
   - Are the main ideas included? Can I delete or combine any of the supporting ideas/details? Can another person read my summary and understand it?

Your assignments require you to do a lot of thinking, but there are many different types of thinking and each is at a different level: recalling, understanding, applying, analyzing, synthesizing, and evaluating. The most basic level is recalling, while the most advanced is evaluating.

Types of Thinking

⇒ Recalling – When you are asked to remember and repeat,
  *listen carefully; take notes,
  *read carefully, and
  *review and study for thorough understanding.
⇒ Understanding – When you are asked to write in your own words,
  *use reading and note-taking strategies (see pages 32-38),
  *rewrite the information in your own words, and
  *explain the information to someone else.
⇒ Applying – When you are asked to demonstrate what you've learned,
  *select the most important main points and details,
  *think about how you could use the information, and
  *organize the information in the best way to answer a question.
⇒ Analyzing – When you are asked to compare and contrast, give reasons, or rank,
  *identify important parts,
  *determine how the parts are related, and
  *write an outline or graphic organizer.
⇒ Synthesizing – When you are asked to combine information to invent, redesign, or predict,
  *combine information with other subjects (study of minerals with space travel),
  *be creative – use material to write a poem, a story, or journal entry, and
  *explore new ideas and models.
⇒ Evaluating – When you are asked to express your own opinion or discuss negatives and positives,
  *learn as much as you can about a subject,
  *recall, review, organize, and analyze what you have learned, and
  *formulate an opinion supported by examples or facts (Sebranek et al. 284-89).

You may want to be a faster thinker, a more logical thinker, or a more creative thinker. Becoming a better thinker takes time and practice. Here are some suggestions.

Becoming a Better Thinker

- Be patient.
  - *Plan, listen, and discuss – don't expect quick, easy solutions.
- Set goals.
  - *Decide what you can do NOW – try a stepping-stone approach.
- Get involved.
  - *Read books, magazines, and newspapers.
  - *Join a club.
  - *Play a team sport.
- Think logically.
  - *Go beyond the first answer that comes to mind.
  - *Consider all possible solutions.
- Ask questions.
  - *"What, who, why/why not, where, how, how much, what if?"
- Be creative.
  - *Look at the world in a new way.
  - *Rewrite, reenact, reinvent.
- Make connections.
  - *Use what you know and apply it to new situations.
  - *Use comparisons, analogies, and metaphors.
  - *See how details are tied together.
- Write ideas down – this helps you remember material longer.
  - *Sort out your thoughts.
  - *Clarify information.
  - *Recognize how you feel about school and/or situations.
    - -You should feel comfortable talking to a teacher or school counselor to express negative feelings ("I can't do this." "I'm afraid that…" "I'm sad that…" "I'm uncomfortable with…") (Sebranek et al. 321).

Memory and recall are essential aspects in the learning process because you are required to recall information to demonstrate what you have learned. The bottom line is that people remember the information they pay attention to.

Memory

What is important to know about memory? How can you boost your memory and recall information? Scientists are not 100% sure how the memory process works; however, recently neuroscientists have made important discoveries that may be useful for you in the classroom.

One of these important scientific discoveries is that the conscious process of memorizing information is complex and involves many different brain systems. In order to memorize information effectively, you must work to activate these systems. For example, memorizing requires focus; therefore, you must capture your brain's attention. One way to accomplish this task is to say aloud what you need to learn. Through your ears sound waves enter your brain's temporal lobes (located on each side of your head next to your ears) and signal your brain to pay attention. Once you have attended to information, another part of your brain works to understand that information; this is called picturing. Say the word "dog" out loud and your brain's visual cortex (located at the back of your head) will "see" an image of a dog faster than you can count. After "picturing" information, your brain's hippocampus (located under your temporal lobes) decides whether to store the information for a long or short time. You can help your hippocampus direct information to long-term memory by associating the new information you are working to learn with information you already know. For instance, you want to memorize the definition for the new vocabulary word "canine," meaning dog. If you consciously attach a specific picture of a dog, maybe your neighbor's brown poodle, to the definition, your chances of remembering the meaning of "canine" improve dramatically. Using color can also help your brain store information long term. Rewrite notes or study for assessments using a minimum of three colors.

Your brain is an amazing instrument. Knowing some of the basics of how your brain processes information will help you learn better and faster. On the following pages, you will find strategies designed to help you consciously retain information; these strategies are based on brain research. Using these "smart" learning techniques will help you fulfill your goal of being the best student you can be (Hanson 1-3, Jenson 99).

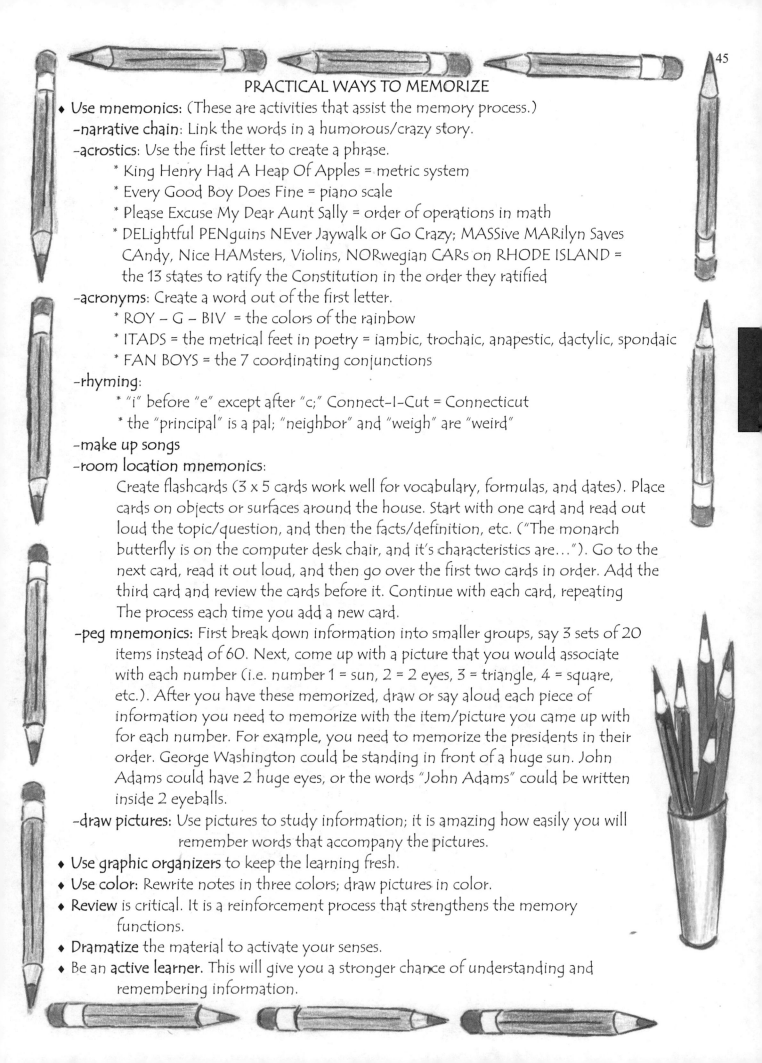

PRACTICAL WAYS TO MEMORIZE

◆ Use mnemonics: (These are activities that assist the memory process.)

-narrative chain: Link the words in a humorous/crazy story.

-acrostics: Use the first letter to create a phrase.
* King Henry Had A Heap Of Apples = metric system
* Every Good Boy Does Fine = piano scale
* Please Excuse My Dear Aunt Sally = order of operations in math
* DELightful PENguins NEver Jaywalk or Go Crazy; MASSive MARilyn Saves CAndy, Nice HAMsters, Violins, NORwegian CARs on RHODE ISLAND = the 13 states to ratify the Constitution in the order they ratified

-acronyms: Create a word out of the first letter.
* ROY – G – BIV = the colors of the rainbow
* ITADS = the metrical feet in poetry = iambic, trochaic, anapestic, dactylic, spondaic
* FAN BOYS = the 7 coordinating conjunctions

-rhyming:
* "i" before "e" except after "c;" Connect-I-Cut = Connecticut
* the "principal" is a pal; "neighbor" and "weigh" are "weird"

-make up songs

-room location mnemonics:
Create flashcards (3 x 5 cards work well for vocabulary, formulas, and dates). Place cards on objects or surfaces around the house. Start with one card and read out loud the topic/question, and then the facts/definition, etc. ("The monarch butterfly is on the computer desk chair, and it's characteristics are…"). Go to the next card, read it out loud, and then go over the first two cards in order. Add the third card and review the cards before it. Continue with each card, repeating The process each time you add a new card.

-peg mnemonics: First break down information into smaller groups, say 3 sets of 20 items instead of 60. Next, come up with a picture that you would associate with each number (i.e. number 1 = sun, 2 = 2 eyes, 3 = triangle, 4 = square, etc.). After you have these memorized, draw or say aloud each piece of information you need to memorize with the item/picture you came up with for each number. For example, you need to memorize the presidents in their order. George Washington could be standing in front of a huge sun. John Adams could have 2 huge eyes, or the words "John Adams" could be written inside 2 eyeballs.

-draw pictures: Use pictures to study information; it is amazing how easily you will remember words that accompany the pictures.

◆ Use graphic organizers to keep the learning fresh.

◆ Use color: Rewrite notes in three colors; draw pictures in color.

◆ Review is critical. It is a reinforcement process that strengthens the memory functions.

◆ Dramatize the material to activate your senses.

◆ Be an active learner. This will give you a stronger chance of understanding and remembering information.

46

While using mnemonics,
- **get emotionally involved** with the information (think about the information so it makes you feel happy or sad).
- remember to sustain a **positive attitude.** Remind yourself, "Yes, I can!"
- remember that a **relaxed learner** is a ready learner.
- **celebrate your mistakes** so you can learn from them, not fear them.
- **consider movement.** While rehearsing and repeating important information, take some steps around the room (for example, if you have three facts to support a main idea, take a step as you say aloud each fact).
- say "Got it!" to yourself after memorizing each piece. This gives a clean ending signal to the brain making recall easier.

The key is to make information stick for a long time.
- **Reviewing helps you retain** information longer. Even if you do not know if there is a test coming up, it is important that you review material from your classes each night. On consecutive days, quickly go over what you reviewed the night before and then review the new material. Repeat each night. You will find that you will not need to spend as much time studying the night before a test.

Activity
The following is a list of the first seven presidents.
Create a humorous or odd narrative chain (story)
to help you remember the names in date order.
George Washington, John Adams, Thomas Jefferson,
James Madison, James Monroe, John Quincy Adams, Andrew Jackson

Would you believe that research shows that after one week, students retain only about 5% of what they hear, 10% of what they read, and between 20-30% of what they hear and see? However, students retain much more of what they practice (75%) and what they teach others or use immediately (90%) (Magnesen 25).

How do you learn to spell a word like <u>government</u> or a difficult word like <u>onomatopoeia</u>? Use the following technique for these trickier words or for even two-syllable words.
1. Cut a thin strip of paper approximately 1 1/2" by 8."
2. Decide how to divide your word, usually in syllables (1 syllable words can be divided into sections with at least 2 letters). Fold your paper into sections depending on how you divided the word. For *onomatopoeia,* fold the paper into 6 sections ("on," "o," "mat," "o," "poe," "ia").
3. Choose 2 bright colors. With the first color, write "on" in the first "box."
4. Hold the paper above your head, but only look up with your eyes (keep face forward). Say the letters to yourself for 7 seconds.
5. Repeat #3 and #4 for each of the sections, rotating the 2 colors ("o," "mat," "o," "poe," "ia").
6. Now spell each section out of order (5th: "poe," 1st: "on," 6th: "ia," 3rd: "mat," 2nd: "o," 4th: "o").
7. Spell the word backwards ("aieopotamono").
8. NOW spell it forwards! Do you see the 2 colors when you spell the word?

Used by permission of Quantum Learning/SuperCamp, www.quantumlearning.com

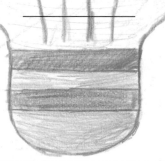

Activity

You have five minutes for the following activity. First, decide upon the mnemonic strategy you prefer. Then, **memorize** the list. After five minutes, write down as many words as you recall on a separate piece of paper. The words can be in any order.

Now score your list:

_____

lettuce	cone	vegetable	leaf
adjustment	dig	harvest	agriculture
growth	pesticides	plow	objective
stand	seed	tractor	root
Purple Leaf basil	row	crop	stem

(Hanson 9)

Reflections: Take a minute to consider your score. Give three to four reasons your strategy worked or did not work.

_____

_____

_____

_____

_____

_____

_____

_____

_____

_____

_____

Share with someone the technique you used to memorize the words above and your reflections.

Ways to Improve Concentration

At **HOME:**
  *Study in a quiet place.
    -Refocus when "mini vacations" intrude.
  *Remove all distractions.
    -Turn off the TV.
    -Leave the phone alone.
    -Stay away from the computer.
    -Ask parent(s) to help remove distractions.
  *Play music that is soothing to help you focus (not for everyone).
  *Take short breaks.
  *Monitor study time – keep a clock handy.
  *Push yourself to finish each assignment.
  *Imagine that the work is personally important to you.
  *Stop working when tired.

At **SCHOOL:**
  *Sit near the front of the room, if possible.
  *Stay away from talkative friends.
  *Have everything you need for the class.
  *Tell yourself "This Is It" when you enter the room.
    -Focus on the teacher.
    -Pay close attention to what is said/done.
    -Take notes, especially instructions or additions/changes to
      homework.

Did you know that reciting material out loud helps you remember it longer?

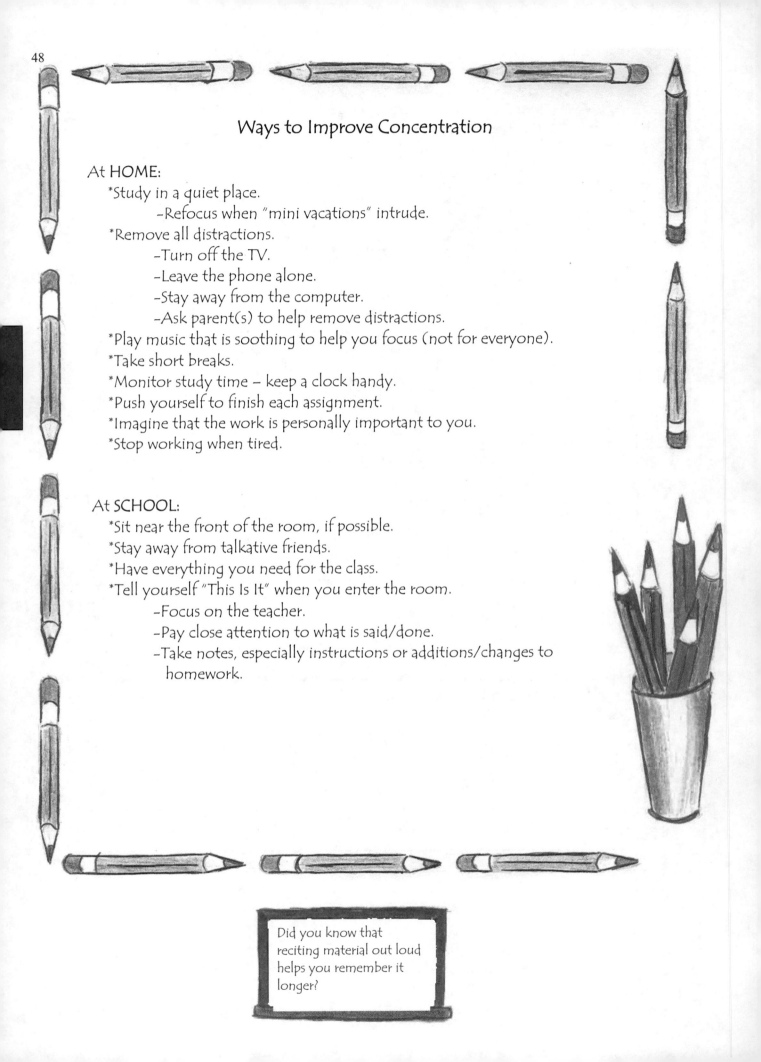

Ways to Cure Carelessness

♦ Think ahead for each class.
♦ Be prepared.
♦ Be organized.
♦ Be prompt – don't wait for the 2nd bell!
♦ <u>Always</u> check your work before turning it in.
♦ <u>Always</u> proofread essays, research papers, and projects.
    -Check spelling, grammar, and flow.
♦ Be neat.
    -Write slowly enough to have legible handwriting or type
      your work.
    -Don't cram it all together.
♦ Pay attention to details.

Four Causes of Carelessness

♦ Rushing to get work done
♦ Not managing your time to be able to check for accuracy
♦ Going off on tangents
♦ Not communicating a need for help

Reflections: List four characteristics of a successful student you know. How are you the same or different?

_____
_____
_____
_____
_____
_____
_____
_____
_____
_____
_____
_____

Activity
Write yourself an encouraging paragraph
discussing the strategies that you would incorporate
into your new study routine.

Know when you are most productive and do challenging assignments during that time. Make time for relaxation and exercise – you need a healthy balance between work and play. Having trouble getting started on your homework? Start it at the same time and place each day – this avoids waiting until you are 'in the mood.' Most likely you already know about setting goals and organizing your time, but there is always room for improvement.

TIME MANAGEMENT TIPS

To help manage your time at HOME:

- Get into a homework routine.
- Start by doing the most difficult assignment(s) first.
- Take a 5 minute break each 30 minutes.
    - Get a drink. – Walk the dog.
    - Eat a snack. – Look at a magazine.
    - Exercise.   – Call a friend for homework help, if needed.
- Check each assignment in your planner as you finish – be mindful of multiple assignments in a class.
- Spend time getting started on/continuing assignments due at a later date.
- Prepare for/work on projects, research papers, or read novels.
- If on a team or in another activity, do some of that night's homework the night before.
- Before bedtime, review subjects that are most difficult for you or review test material.
- Read something you enjoy each day.

While playing sports, remember your sunscreen. Harmful sunrays between 10 a.m. and 4 p.m. can cause skin cancer. Wear sunglasses and a hat, too!

To help manage your time at **SCHOOL**:

- Use your academic planner in every class.
- Keep all subject materials organized so that you have everything you need when you enter the classroom.
- Attend extra help/review sessions or schedule a session with your teacher.
- Be sure you understand how to do each assignment before leaving class.
- In case you miss school:

  −have a homework pal who will collect handouts for you, explain each assignment, and share class notes.

  −ask your teacher in the beginning of a school year how you can find out about missed work (many schools have electronic posting or allow students to e-mail a teacher or even call a teacher at home).

DOING HOMEWORK

- Prepare your workspace.
  - −Gather all the materials you will need.
- Prioritize your assignments.
  - −Light night of homework:
    - 1) Take 5-10 minute breaks between subject assignments.
    - 2) Take a longer break at the halfway point − practice your instrument, etc.
  - −Heavy night of homework:
    - 1) Study for test(s)/quiz(zes) first.
    - 2) Take a 10-15 minute break; practice your instrument, etc.
    - 3) Complete other assignments with breaks in between.
    - 4) Review for test(s)/quiz(zes) a couple of times between other subjects and then before bedtime.
- Allow for breaks.
- Take time each night to read over class notes to help you fully understand related material prior to the next assessment.
- Have your homework pal's phone number handy.
- If you choose to study with a friend, decide beforehand what you'll cover.
  - −Stay focused.   −Quiz each other.
- Reward yourself at the end with a fun activity or relaxing moment.
- Always strive to turn in assignments on time.

Get up and move! Movement brings much needed oxygen to your muscles and brain. Even just standing up can help you refocus.

WHAT AM I DOING WRONG?

1. How do I get started?
    - Make a list.
    - Break the tasks into doable chunks (each task is about 15-20 minutes of work.
    - Do the most challenging assignment first and least challenging last.
2. I have too much to study and too little time.
    - Focus on main topics/skills.
    - Organize and preview.
3. My assignments are boring.
    - Attack the material.
    - Look for interesting facts and take notes or summarize.
    - Underline important information.
    - Discuss the material with your homework pal or your parents.
    - Make up a story using the material to be learned.
4. I can't get this to really make sense!
    - Link new material to something you already know or something in the present.
    - Chunk the material – divide large amounts of material into related and ordered sections.
    - Use Mnemonics – any memory-assisting technique (see pages 44-46).
    - Read the material into a tape recorder and then play it back.
        * Talk out loud to yourself.
    - Think about why you are reading – what is the goal of the section?
    - Preview pictures, graphs, and words in bold type.
    - Use the KWL Strategy or other graphic organizer.
        * What do I know?
        * What do I need/want to know?
        * What have I learned?
    - Create flashcards or a match game.
    - Create lists with two columns.
        * Write one set of facts on one side of the paper and the related facts on the other – fold the paper in half; use a highlighter to mark what you know well.
    - Rewrite, Rewrite.
        * Some visual or kinesthetic learners may need to write material over a number of times.
    - Walk around the house (or other activity) reading notes out loud if you are a kinesthetic learner.
5. I hope I get it.
    - Create your own quiz or test on the material.
    - Ask your homework pal or parent to quiz you.
6. I can't remember it all.
    - Organize the information.
    - Make up an outline or other graphic organizer (see pages 34-38).

Rewrite, draw pictures, make up a song, or create a graphic organizer.

7. I thought I knew it!

-Review new material every day for each class.

-Look at the questions at the end of the chapter or section.

-Organize the material in a different way and restudy (you can't over study).

8. I want to study in bed or a cozy chair.

-For homework: You should be sitting up at a desk, table, floor, or bed.

-For quizzes/tests: Sit in a straight-backed chair as if taking the assessment.

9. I like to wait until the night before a test to review.

-Start studying now! Make up those flashcards, songs, stories early.

-Recall increases when study time is spread out over time.

10. I like to stay up late until I know it.

-Take short breaks to ward off mental exhaustion.

-Review material ahead of time.

-Exercise during the day, find time for quiet reflection, and remember to breathe.

-Eat healthy meals and snacks, and monitor your daily schedule to ensure 8 hours of sleep/day ("Ten Traps," sec. 3).

Activity

Use the first letters of the countries in Central America to create a humorous phrase to remember them:

Belize, Guatemala, El Salvador, Honduras, Nicaragua, Costa Rica, and Panama

_____

_____

_____

_____

_____

_____

Do your teachers complain they can't read your handwriting??

⇨ Slow down! Don't rush through your work.

⇨ Be creative!

-Come up with a new style of writing (i.e. mix cursive and print).

⇨ Type your homework on a word processor.

⇨ Use an appropriate and comfortable writing utensil.

MANAGING STRESS

⇨ Types of stress
  "Good Stress" – stress that motivates and/or increases productivity
    *Getting psyched up to meet a challenge
    *Competing in a sport
    *Performing in a play or concert
    *Talking in front of your peers
  "Bad stress" – stress that adversely affects performance
    Stress can present different symptoms:
    *Anger
    *Headaches
    *Loss of sleep
    *Eating too much or too little
    *Shutting down

⇨ Causes of stress:
    *Doing poorly in school   *Doing something you know is wrong
    *Peer pressure   *High expectations by you or a parent
    *Family issues   *Performing in front of others
    *Moving

⇨ Symptoms of stress overload:
    *Unusual mood swings   *Overdoing an activity
    *Disinterest in school   *Test anxiety
    *Loss of concentration   *Low self-esteem
    *Withdrawal from activities/friends/family   *Sleeping too much

⇨ **Ways to reduce stress:**
    *Get to the root of the problem.
    *Temporarily avoid the problem through exercise, relaxation, reading, etc.
    *Eat healthy.
    *Get some exercise.
    *Stay away from negative influences.
        - Sarcastic "friends" are not helpful.
        - Don't let social life get in the way.
        - Forgive yourself.
        - Look for a new solution.
    *Ask for advice.
        -Don't give in to a negative inner voice.
        -Talk to a friend, teacher, or school counselor.
    *Learn from your mistakes.
    *Cut back on activities if time is stretched too thin.
    *Do journal writing about your feelings/thoughts.
    *Read something that you enjoy.
    *Remember to take a few deep breaths before any stressful event (i.e. a test).
        -Come up with positive jingles to diminish negative thoughts ("If I do
        poorly on this test, the world won't end!" "I can do this!").

> Praise yourself at the end of each day for goals met. Say only kind words and do only kind acts. Live the Golden Rule!

(continued....)

⇨ Managing Stress Outside of School:

From parents:

*Be sure that you <u>are</u> doing your best.

*Communication – show your parents the new techniques you are trying in order to improve; discuss the pressure you are feeling.

*Give yourself affirmations – congratulate yourself on your successes no matter how small.

From yourself:

*Don't procrastinate.

*Refocus when you find you are daydreaming during homework or in class.

*Put academic success before your social life.

*Be responsible for your success (Griswold 96).

Reflections: Look back on what you have just read.
Write two examples of "good stress" you anticipate encountering this school year.

1. _____
2. _____

Write two examples of "bad stress" you may encounter this school year.

1. _____
2. _____

List five techniques you might use to cope with the stresses you may encounter.

1. _____
2. _____
3. _____
4. _____
5. _____

After reading the message below on the whiteboard, create two affirmations that will help you.

1. _____
2. _____

Research says that it takes ten affirmations to override one negative belief!

Relaxation Technique

Lie down.

Close your eyes.

Put your hands over your stomach. Take a deep breath through your nose.

Slowly release your breath out of your mouth and feel your hands sink.

Breathe in again. Breathe out. Pause.

Breathe in. Breathe out. Pause.

Keep the rest of your body relaxed – now clench your right fist tightly.

Hold for five seconds. Pause.

Relax.

Do the same with your left fist for five seconds.

Now do the same tensing/pause/relaxing technique with

> Biceps
> Forehead
> Teeth
> Shoulders
> Back
> Toes

Now, try to keep your mind blank and concentrate on relaxation.

Lie peacefully for one or two moments.

Get back to work (Griswold 98)!!

Relax....

Taking quizzes and tests can be a nerve-wracking experience if you are not prepared. If you are organized, attentive, and prepared, taking quizzes and tests can be a rewarding experience. Let's see how you can become better equipped for this experience.

Preparing for Tests and Exams

When the Test/Exam is announced:
- make sure you understand what the test/exam will cover.
- determine what <u>kind</u> of test will it be- objective, short essay, long essay, etc.
- mark the date in your academic planner.
- prepare a study schedule – prepare a few days before.
- review notes/homework to see if you have any questions.
- make sure that you are not missing any information.

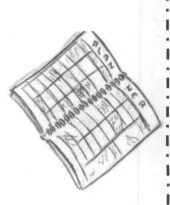

When studying for the Test/Exam:
- prepare summary sheets, outlines, and flash cards according to your learning preference.
- spend several nights before the test making final notes and reviewing in chunks.
- use mnemonics (see pages 44-46).
- stress important areas in your review:
     *points emphasized by the teacher;
     *areas highlighted in your text and notes;
     *questions from study guides, past quizzes, and chapter reviews;
     *review all material. Focus particularly on the difficult parts or parts about which you are unsure.

★Especially for Exams
- Last-minute cramming usually does not help.
- Develop a calm, logical approach to studying.
     *Don't get caught up in any panic situation created by other students.
- If you study with a peer, choose someone with a calm, orderly approach.
- Use your planner to divide up time for studying for each of your exams.
- Schedule more time for subjects in which you are more challenged.
- Study for difficult subjects during times of the day when you feel the most alert.
- Study your strong subjects every other day.
- Develop an "order of attack" for each subject (Griswold 113-14). (continued…)

-Work from your exam review sheet.
    *Pull out notes and quizzes/tests.
    *Write up answers to the review sheet questions using this material.
-Practice reading exam questions by looking over questions from tests.
-Use the last hours before an exam to review those areas in which you are the weakest.
-Get plenty of sleep--fatigue can destroy concentration.

Taking Quizzes and Tests

-Get to class with time to sharpen your pencil or find a pen you like.
-Listen carefully to directions – ask questions if needed.
-Look over the entire test first - underline key words in the directions for each section.
-Budget your time for each section.
-Answer the questions you know first.
-Circle or underline key words in multiple choice, true/false, and matching questions.
-Clearly mark questions that you need to return to.
-Leave time at the end to review - reread directions and check your answers.
-Don't waste a lot of time struggling over parts you do not know well.
-Use extra time to check for careless errors and completeness of answers.

Multiple-choice questions:
  -Eliminate obvious incorrect answers.
  -Make a logical guess between the remaining options.

True/False questions:
  -Answer "true" only if every part of the statement is true.
  -Words like "all", "never", or "always" usually suggest the statement is false.

Matching:
  -Skip around and answer those you know well first.
  -Write possible choices next to the remaining statements.
  -Look closely at key words.

Essays:
  -Underline key words in the directions.
  -Quickly outline your ideas.
  -Return to the question to refocus your thoughts.
  -Be as neat as possible.
  -Write exactly what the question asks for - it can be a waste
    of time to write more than is asked for.
  -Proofread your essay.

When the Test is Returned

-Make corrections if possible.
-Correct errors in your notes.
-Make an appointment with your teacher to discuss if:
    ⇨ you are confused.
    ⇨ your grade is low.
    ⇨ your grade is lower than usual for you.

Activity

This example shows how to answer to an essay question on a test.
As you read this, <u>underline key words</u> in the <u>question</u>
and in the <u>thesis (topic) statement</u>.

Example:

Q: Many historians state that the Great Depression of the 1930s was caused partially by the spending habits of the American people during the 1920s. In a well written paragraph, explain how the spending habits of the 1920s led to the Great Depression.

T.S.: The Americans' spending habits of the 1920s contributed to the development of the Great Depression of the 1930s.

1. To write your essay, first form your thesis (topic) statement. You could reword the question or use part of it.
2. Next, stop and think about the question; list or cluster what you might include in your answer (on back of another page). The thesis (topic) statement directs your ideas. You must also consider the order of your supporting ideas.
3. Now write the essay, occasionally looking back at the instructions and the question.
4. Proofread your essay. Is it clear and does it answer the question?

Reflections: Reflect on whether this task was easy or difficult for you.

_____

_____

_____

_____

_____

_____

_____

_____

_____

_____

_____

_____

_____

_____

APPENDIX

Being a successful student takes more than academic ability. It requires social skills, too. Here are a few tips every student should know.

LIFE SKILLS

o   Get Organized.
  ⇨ Keep your locker neat and clean.
  ⇨ Be a good steward of your school's grounds
     (means that you do not drop trash
     and pick up trash when you see it).

o   Get to Know Your Teachers.
  ⇨ Greet them each day.
  ⇨ Ask questions.
  ⇨ Take advantage of extra help.

o   Become a Responsible Student.
  ⇨ Complete your work on time.
  ⇨ Be on time at the start of school each day and for each class.
  ⇨ Focus during class – avoid social conversations during class discussions.

o   Make Friends.
  ⇨ Be friendly, kind, and polite.
  ⇨ Be an active listener.
  ⇨ Be inclusive.
  ⇨ Make the commitment NOT to gossip.
  ⇨ Treat others as you would want to be treated.
  ⇨ Be a peacemaker and help mediate problems between classmates (listen to both
     sides and help those in conflict reach a compromise).
  ⇨ Remember – building good friendships may take time.

Life Skills Golden Rules
  ⇨ Be respectful.
  ⇨ Be kind to others.
  ⇨ Listen when others are speaking.
  ⇨ Be willing to let go of first impressions (don't judge).

Positive Character Traits

⇨ Cooperation
⇨ Effective communication ("I" messages)
⇨ Empathy – consider others' feelings
⇨ Fairness
⇨ Honesty
⇨ Respect differences
⇨ Kindness
⇨ Sensitivity

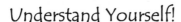

Understand Yourself!

What are Virtues?

Virtues are principles people CHOOSE to live by.
Virtues INFLUENCE people's CHOICES and ACTIONS.

What are Emotions?

Emotions are a way to express feelings.
Everyone expresses emotions differently.

Are you a PROactive or REactive person?

Proactive:	Reactive:
⇨ choices based upon virtues	⇨ choices based upon impulses
⇨ thinking before acting	⇨ inability to control oneself

(Covey 49-51)

Statements About Conflict

Conflict is a part of everyday life.
Conflict can
-be handled in positive or negative ways.
-have either creative or destructive results.
-be a positive force for personal growth and social change.

Most conflicts involve an attempt to meet
the BASIC needs of:
-belonging,
-power,
-freedom, or
-fun (Schrumpf et al. 25).

Activity

First, read the whiteboard below. Then, change the response "Whatever!" into a positive phrase.

_____

_____

_____

_____

_____

_____

Use positive body language and phrasing! Be aware of your body language to teachers and avoid sighing, rolling your eyes, snickering, etc. Your phrasing influences the student-teacher relationship. View your teacher as an academic coach, one who works with you to reach your academic goals.

A computer is very useful for homework, projects, games, and research. The Internet can be an efficient use of time or another way to waste time. Yes, chat rooms and games can be fun, but the Internet has a wealth of information.

COMPUTERS AND WRITING

USING THE INTERNET

⇨ **Be patient** – there is so much information; it may take you time to find the right resources for you.

⇨ **Learn how to judge** what information is accurate and responsible – do not use papers written by students to cite as a source; find their sources to use for yourself.

⇨ **"Surfing" the Net**
  1. Stay focused on your specific task.
  2. Examine your web source.
    –Educational, government, and most business sites are very reliable.
    –Question private sites.
    –If multiple sources say the same thing, most likely the information is correct.
    –Ask a parent, teacher, or media specialist to help you judge the information.
  3. Preserve your privacy.
    –Don't give out personal information (address, phone number, or personal details about you–check with a parent or teacher first); don't give out your password.
  4. Protect yourself.
    –If you accidentally encounter an offensive site, quickly delete it and report it; close "spammed" messages.
  5. Follow rules of "netiquette."
    –Don't SHOUT (using all capitals) and don't use inappropriate language (Sebranek et al. 268-9).

(continued…)

USING THE LIBRARY

⇨ Search the card catalog by title, author's last name, or subject.
  -Each card will have a call number (where to find the book
    on the shelf).
⇨ Search the computer catalog by title, author's last name, or
    subject.
⇨ Keep a list of your sources. Include title, author(s) or editor(s), publishing company
    and city where published, and date of last publication (all found on first
    couple of pages).

WRITING AN ESSAY OR RESEARCH PAPER

The following was written using the guidelines written in the OWL Online Writing Lab:
  (http://owl.english.purdue.edu)

AN OVERVIEW:

You will be assigned various papers at school requiring you to include information from an established source or other valid materials. The source could be a novel, the internet, or any other work from which you borrow ideas. In order to combine their words with your thoughts or ideas, you will need to use three strategies: _summarization_, _paraphrasing_, _and/or_ _quotations_. After you use your source with one (or more) of these three strategies, you will also need to give credit to the author.

Summarizing: This strategy is used to put the main idea(s) of one or more authors into your own words. You only include the main points of the research. Summarized ideas do not have to be written in the same order as the main points from the original source. Summaries are much shorter than the original and give a broad overview of your resource(s). You must give credit for information in your summary because it contains key words or ideas taken from a source or collection of sources.

Paraphrasing: This strategy is used to put the words of an author into your own words. You are rephrasing the words of an author, and you are not adding your opinion. Translate or restate the author's words into your own words. First, reread the selection several times until you understand it, then restate it in your own words. Paraphrasing can be used when the original words are difficult to understand or the vocabulary is particularly complex. Writing that is paraphrased is often slightly shorter than the original work. You must give credit in your text and in your Works Cited page for information that is written in your own words but contains key words or ideas taken from a source. This is because they are not your own ideas, but rather those of the author you referenced.

Quotations: This strategy is used to copy the exact words of an author **word for word**. You must give credit within your text and in the Works Cited page for information quoted directly from another source. Quotations should be used minimally (DO NOT quote if you can summarize or paraphrase).

GETTING STARTED:

⇨Choose a topic and begin researching by reading (you may need to restrict your topic or refine it).

⇨Start writing the bibliography for the Works Cited page on 3x5" cards.

⇨Read the source, highlighting, or underlining key points and main ideas.

⇨As you start your research notes, be sure to mark whether you are summarizing, paraphrasing, and/or using direct quotes as part of your essay or paper.

⇨Use note cards or half sheets of paper to write notes for your essay or paper. Be sure to write the name of the source and page number on each card or sheet.

⇨Once you have taken all of your notes, write an outline. This outline helps to organize your ideas and your research. It only gives a general description of each paragraph. Your outline can be in sentence or topic structure.

> First:
> - **Develop** your **thesis** statement or paragraph.
>
> Then:
> - **Brainstorm**: List all the ideas you want to include.
> - **Organize**: Group related ideas from your research together.
> - **Order**: You may need to list supporting details from general to specific.

(For more information, see OWL™ Online Writing Lab : http://owl.english.purdue.edu/handouts/)

WRITING THE PAPER:

To help you learn and for simplicity's sake, we chose to include the MLA (Modern Language Association) format. The MLA style uses parenthetical documentation in the body of a research paper or essay to give credit to an author's work. This style helps to keep you, the student writer, responsible for the information you use from your resource(s). And, with proper use of citation, you will keep yourself from plagiarizing.

⇨Plagiarism:
- You can be accused of plagiarism for using the words of your source without citing the source or even if you accidentally use the words of an author of your research.
- Do not copy an author's writing or ideas as if they were your own.
- Do not change just a few words with a thesaurus.
- **Plagiarism can result in severe consequences (possibly an F or zero grade)!**

FIRST DRAFT OF ESSAY:

⇨ Do not use a title page unless requested by your teacher.

⇨ Name, instructor's name, the course title, and the date are listed in order in the top left corner (under the 1" margin). Double-space between each of these.

⇨ Number the pages in the upper right-hand corner, one half inch from the top. Your last name should be written before each page number. Most teachers do not have you number the first page.

⇨ Center your title below the header with your name.

⇨ Double space below the title and then start your essay. Double-space the essay.

See sample on next page.

Sample:

```
                                                                    Doe 1


   John Doe

   Mrs. June Smith

   English 7

   5 April 2005

                                    Title

      Start paper here...
```

CITING THE WORKS OF OTHERS <u>WITHIN</u> YOUR PAPER:

⇨ When you summarize, paraphrase or quote directly in your paper, you need to give credit to each author's ideas <u>within the paper</u>. This is called <u>parenthetical documentation</u> or <u>citation</u>. This is where you give the author's name (or the title of the work) and the page number (or paragraph).

⇨ In this author-page method, the author's name may be given in your paragraph or within the parentheses following the sentence/paragraph/quotation. The page number should always appear within the parentheses. However, with many online sources, you may not have an author or a page number. In that case, you can give the title or a shortened version of the title in quotations within parentheses. Instead of a page number, you can give the paragraph or section [ex: ("A Tale" par. 2).].

Examples:

1. author is stated in your sentence: (42).
2. author is not stated directly: (Patel 42).
3. no author: ("Skeletal System" 21).
4. no author and no page: ("Types of Governments" par. 5).
5. when your source quotes another: (qtd. in "Washington" 5).
6. two authors with same last name: (A. Cohen 12).

   (J. Cohen par. 2). ("par." means electronic source)

7. two works by same author: ("DNA" 25).

   ("Recessive Genes" par. 5).

For more information on using parenthetical citations:
http://www.wisc.edu/writing/Handbook/DocMLACitation.html

ADDITIONAL SUGGESTIONS:
⇨ ALWAYS proofread and revise your work.
- •Are there spelling or grammar mistakes?: Do you need to delete some information that doesn't really fit? Do you need to reorganize your paragraphs?
- •Have a teacher, peer, or parent edit your work. Careful, a peer or a parent can give suggestions, but he/she should not write your paper for you.

WORKS CITED PAGE:
Your Works Cited page appears at the end of your paper on a separate page. Each source you use or cite must be listed in your Works Cited page.
Format:
⇨The title is centered (NO quotation marks or underlining, etc.).
⇨ The first line of each source is flush to the left within the 1" margin. Indent all other lines of the same entry 5 spaces. Double space all lines within each entry.
⇨ Double space between entries.
⇨ Alphabetize your list of works cited.
- •Last name of author is listed first (see example 1). If you have more than one author, invert only the first author's name, follow it with a comma, then continue listing the other authors (see example 2).
- •If you have more than one work by an author, order them alphabetically by title and then use three hyphens in place of the author's name (see example 3).
⇨ If there is no author, alphabetize by the title (see examples 8a and 8c).
⇨ Capitalize each main word in the titles of books, articles, etc.
⇨ Underline or italicize titles of books, journals, magazines, newspapers, and/or films.
⇨ Use quotation marks around the tiles of articles in journals, magazines, and newspapers, and also the titles of short stories, book chapters, poems, and songs.
⇨ There are specific uses of punctuation. When writing your Works Cited page, follow the examples given on the next page very carefully.

Examples:

(1) Book with one author:

Smith, Ann. <u>The Culture of North American Indians</u>. New York: Quality Press, 2005.

(2) Book with more than one author:

Singh, Priya and Pravin Patel. <u>Mathematicians of the Twentieth Century</u>. Boston: Briar Press, 2000.

(3) Two books by same author:

Sousa, David J. <u>Spain</u>. Chicago: Unlimited Press, 1999.

---. <u>The Culture of Spain</u>. New York: McKnight, 2005.

(4) Newspaper article:

[Note: "A5" is the section and page number; for parenthetical citation, write: ("Top Ten" A5).]

Johnson, Sam. "Top Ten Issues of the 2005 Election." <u>New York Times</u> 15 Sept. 2004: A5.

(5) Magazine article:

Sefeed, Azadeh. "Changes in Iran." <u>Time</u> 21 Dec. 2004: 11-14.

(6) Article from a reference book:

"Eli Whitney." Encyclopedia Britannica. 2001 ed.

(7) The Bible (specific editions):

Today's English Version Bible. New York: American Bible Society, 1992.

(8) Basic forms for electronic sources:

It is important to give the date you looked up the site because web postings are often updated.

Example: (Note: to keep web posting within the "< >," insert a space before and after the address.)

Author(s). Name of Page. Date of Posting/Revision. Name of institution/organization connected

with the site. Date of Access <electronic address>.

(a) An article on a web site:

"Facts and Figures About Twisters." <u>Infoplease</u> 2000-2005. Pearson Education 12 June 2005

< http://www.infoplease.com/ipn/.html >.

(b) An article from an electronic database:

Galloway, J. H. "Brazil." <u>World Book Online Reference Center</u>. 2005. World Book, Inc. 12 Mar. 2005

< http://www.aol.svc.worldbook.aol.com >.

(c) An article from a reference database on CD-ROM:

"Mangroves." <u>Encarta</u>. CD-ROM. Seattle: Microsoft, 2000.

For more information: http://owl.english.purdue.edu/handouts/print/research

Cite your sources!!

Effort makes the difference!

Remember, as you mature and grow, your learning styles and preferences will change. Refer to this handbook throughout your middle school years as needed. It would be a good idea at the beginning of each school year to retake the inventories at the front of the handbook.

GLOSSARY

> **Acrostics.** A composition usually in verse in which sets of letters (as the initial or final letters of the lines) taken in order form a word or phrase or a regular sequence of letters of the alphabet.

> **Active learner.** A focused and involved student who is attentive to what he or she is trying to learn.

> **Anagram.** A word or phrase made by transposing the letters of another word or phrase.

> **Auditory learner.** A person whose learning preference is listening/hearing information.

> **Brain hemispheres.** There are two cerebral hemispheres in the human brain: the left and the right. They are connected by bundles of nerve fibers called the corpus callosum.

> **Combination learner.** A person who uses two or more learning preferences somewhat equally when mastering information.

> **Cramming.** An ineffective method of studying which occurs when a student attempts to memorize a great deal of information at one time or at the last minute.

> **Declarative/Explicit memory.** A form of memory that addresses the mind's understanding of connections, meanings, or relationships among new and old information. It is based on both a creative and an analytic capacity to see relationships.

> **Episodic memory.** A form of memory and learning that is prompted by the particular location or circumstance. Strong sensory experiences including sights, sounds, smells, taste, and touch magnify it.

> **Existential.** A multiple intelligence identified by Dr. Howard Gardner. A student who demonstrates an ability and sensitivity to consider deep questions about human existence, such as the meaning of life, death, and creation.

> **Graphic organizers.** A visual tool used to represent information that is about to be or just was learned.

> *Inspiration*®. A computer software program that provides the tools needed to present ideas or concepts in the form of diagrams. It is ideal when a learner is making a graphic organizer.

> **Instrument.** A formal series of questions used to reveal information about an individual.

> **Intelligence.** The ability to learn or understand or to deal with new or trying situations by using skills of reason.

> **Interpersonal/People smart.** A multiple intelligence identified by Dr. Howard Gardner. A student whose intellect demonstrates an ability to make and maintain friends easily, is

sensitive to the feelings and moods of others, is a good mediator, leader and organizer, and can see things from another's perspective.

- ➤ **Intrapersonal/Self smart.** A multiple intelligence identified by Dr. Howard Gardner. A student who demonstrates an ability to understand feelings, strengths, ideas, values and beliefs, is able to create and fulfill objectives, and benefits from private time to think and reflect.

- ➤ **Kinesthetic/Body smart.** A multiple intelligence identified by Dr. Howard Gardner. A student who demonstrates an ability to unite body and mind for better physical performance, has good motor skills, and can use the body as a means of self expression, such as dancing, athletics, and acting.

- ➤ **Kinesthetic learner.** A person whose learning preference is a hands-on manipulation of information.

- ➤ **KWL chart.** An effective study/reading strategy to help the student enhance or further understand a topic.

- ➤ **Logical/Mathematical.** A multiple intelligence identified by Dr. Howard Gardner. A student who demonstrates strong ability with numbers, computations, quantifying, sequencing, analyzing, evaluating, synthesizing, and applying. These students think in numbers, abstract symbols, algorithms, and logical sequences.

- ➤ **Mind-mapping/Webbing.** An effective study/reading strategy to help the student organize critical information. When creating a mind-map/web, the student starts with the name of the subject in the middle of the web/mind-map and branches the supporting details from there.

- ➤ **Mnemonics.** Techniques for improving the memory.

- ➤ **Multiple intelligences.** A theory presented by Dr. Howard Gardner. According to the research, all human beings have at least eight different types of intelligence. Individuals have some intelligences that are more highly developed than others due to personal background and age.

- ➤ **Musical/Rhythmic.** A multiple intelligence identified by Dr. Howard Gardner. A student who demonstrates an ability to communicate or gain understanding from music, or listen to music regularly, play an instrument or sing, or determine pitch, timbre, timing, tone and rhythm of sounds.

- ➤ **Naturalist.** A multiple intelligence identified by Dr. Howard Gardner. A student who demonstrates a strong understanding of the natural world.

- ➤ **Objective list.** A list (self-generated or required) toward which effort is directed: an aim, goal, or end of action.

- **Paraphrasing.** Restating or rephrasing an author's words into your own words.

- **Parenthetical citation/documentation.** Referencing a source within your writing using parentheses.

- **Passive learner.** A non-involved student who is not attentive to what he or she is trying to learn.

- **Process list.** A list created during note-taking that shows the steps, or stages, in the order in which they are presented in the reading, lecture, etc.

- **Pun.** The usually humorous use of a word in such a way as to suggest two or more of its meanings or the meaning of another word similar in sound.

- **Semantic memory.** Part of the declarative memory system that includes names, facts, figures, and textbook information.

- **Spoonerism.** A transposition of initial sounds of two or more words (as in *tons of soil* for *sons of toil*).

- **SQ3R.** A study-reading strategy to enrich the reader's understanding for assigned reading. Involves surveying, question making, reading, reciting and reviewing; coined by F. P. Robinson (1946) in <u>Effective Study</u>.

- **Stress relaxation.** Specific exercises designed to help relieve an individual's level of stress or anxiety.

- **Study Skills.** Techniques used by a learner to acquire and remember new information.

- **Summarizing.** The process of writing in your own words a broad overview of an author's main ideas.

- **Table organizer.** A graphic organizer created to help a person sort out the important details of selected information.

- **Time line.** A type of graphic organizer that gives a learner an overview of critical historical information by presenting a combination of dates and events in chronological order.

- **Visual/Spatial.** A multiple intelligence identified by Dr. Howard Gardner. A student who demonstrates an ability to think and create images and pictures, and to visualize accurately and abstractly.

- **Visual learner.** A person whose learning preference is seeing information.

- **Verbal/Linguistic.** A multiple intelligence identified by Dr. Howard Gardner. A student who demonstrates well-developed verbal skills and an ability to recognize sounds, meanings, and the rhythm of words.

Works Cited

Armstrong, Thomas. <u>Multiple Intelligences In the Classroom</u>. Alexandria: Association for Supervision and Curriculum Development, 1994.

Covey, Sean. <u>The 7 Habits of Highly Effective Teens</u>. New York: Fireside, 1998.

DePorter, Bobbi, Mark Reardon, and Sarah Singer-Nourie. <u>Quantum Teaching</u>. Needham Heights: Allyn and Bacon, A Viacom Company, 1999.

---. "My Learning Profile." 2003 Supercamp notebook. The Learning Forum, Incorporated. Wake Forest University, Winston-Salem. 27 July 2003.

Griswold, David H. <u>How To Study</u>. 2nd ed. White Plains: Longman Publishing Group, 1994.

Hanson, J. Robert. "Memory Strategy For Student Learning." J. Robert Hanson & Associates, Incorporated. Association for Supervision and Curriculum Development, Chicago. July 1998.

Inspiration® Inspiration Software®, Incorporated. Site License. 10 July 2003.

Jenson, Eric. <u>Teaching With the Brain in Mind</u>. Alexandria: Association for Supervision and Curriculum Development, 1998.

Kagan, Dr. Spencer. <u>Cooperative Learning</u>. San Clemente: Kagan, 1994.

Magnesen, Vernon A. "A Review of Findings from Learning and Memory and Retention Studies." <u>Innovation Abstracts</u>. 5 (1983): 25.

Marzano, Robert, et al. <u>A Handbook for Classroom Instruction That Works</u>. Alexandria: Association for Supervision and Curriculum Development, 2001.

McKenzie, Walter. "Multiple Intelligences Survey-How Are You Smart?" <u>Surfaquarium</u>. 1999. Surfaquarium. 20 June 2003 <http://surfaquarium.com/im.htm>.

Purdue University Online Writing Lab (OWL). <u>Using Modern Language Association (MLA) Format</u>. 2004. 11 June 2005 <http://owl.english.purdue.edu>.

Schrumpf, Fred, et al. <u>Conflict Resolution in School</u>. Champaign: Research Press, 1997.

Sebranek, Patrick, Dave Kemper, and Verne Meyer. <u>Write Source 2000: A Guide to Writing, Thinking, and Learning.</u> Wilmington: Great Source Education Group, 1999.

---. <u>Write Source 2000: A Guide to Writing, Thinking, and Learning</u>. Wilmington: D.C. Heath and Company, 1995.

"Study Skills Survey." 2003. <u>University Minnesota Duluth</u>. 13 June 2003 <www.d.umn.edu/student/cgi/embp.cgi/student/embpstudy_skills.htm>.

"Improve Your Studying Skills." 2003. <u>CAPS-UNC-Chapel Hill</u>. 13 June 2003 <http://caps.unc.edu/TenTraps.html>.

Notes: _____
_____
_____
_____
_____
_____
_____
_____
_____
_____
_____
_____
_____
_____
_____
_____
_____
_____
_____
_____
_____
_____
_____
_____
_____

Notes: _____

Notes: _____

_____

_____

_____

_____

_____

_____

_____

_____

_____

_____

_____

_____

_____

_____

_____

_____

_____

_____

_____

_____

_____

_____

_____

_____

_____

_____

_____

_____

_____

_____

_____

_____

_____

_____

_____

_____

_____

_____

_____

_____

_____

_____

_____

_____

_____

_____

_____

_____

_____

_____

Notes: _____

Notes: _____
_____
_____
_____
_____
_____
_____
_____
_____
_____
_____
_____
_____
_____
_____
_____
_____
_____
_____
_____
_____
_____
_____
_____
_____
_____
_____
_____
_____
_____
_____
_____
_____
_____
_____
_____
_____
_____
_____
_____
_____
_____
_____
_____
_____
_____
_____

Notes:

Let's find out your learning preference. Are you a VISUAL, AUDITORY, or KINESTHETIC learner, or are you a COMBINATION? First, check the appropriate box for each question. Then, add up your checks going down the column, multiply the total by the number given, and add up the totals for each section. After you have answered the questions for all three sections, use the totals to graph your results.

LEARNING STYLES PROFILE
WHAT TYPE OF LEARNER ARE YOU?

VISUAL – AUDITORY – KINESTHETIC (V-A-K) ASSESSMENT
Mark the appropriate box for each question. Tally your score for each section.

VISUAL

	often	sometimes	seldom
◆ Are you neat and orderly?	☐	☐	☐
◆ Do you speak quickly?	☐	☐	☐
◆ Are you a good long-range planner and organizer?	☐	☐	☐
◆ Are you a good speller and can you actually see the words in your mind?	☐	☐	☐
◆ Do you remember what was seen rather than heard?	☐	☐	☐
◆ Do you memorize by visual association?	☐	☐	☐
◆ Do you have trouble remembering verbal instructions unless they are written down, and do you often ask people to repeat themselves?	☐	☐	☐
◆ Would you rather read than be read to?	☐	☐	☐
◆ Do you doodle during phone conversations/class/meetings?	☐	☐	☐
◆ Would you rather do a demonstration than make a speech?	☐	☐	☐
◆ Do you like art more than music?	☐	☐	☐
◆ Do you know what to say but can't think of the right words?	☐	☐	☐

subtotals = _____   _____   _____

x 2   x 1   x 0

totals = _____ + _____ + _____

= _____

AUDITORY

	often	sometimes	seldom
♦ Do you speak to yourself while working?	☐	☐	☐
♦ Are you easily distracted by noise?	☐	☐	☐
♦ Do you move your lips/pronounce the words as you read?	☐	☐	☐
♦ Do you enjoy reading aloud and listening?	☐	☐	☐
♦ Can you repeat back and mimic tone, pitch, and timbre?	☐	☐	☐
♦ Do you find writing difficult, but are better at telling?	☐	☐	☐
♦ Do you speak in rhythmic patterns?	☐	☐	☐
♦ Do you think you're an eloquent speaker?	☐	☐	☐
♦ Do you like music more than art?	☐	☐	☐
♦ Do you learn by listening and remember what was discussed rather than seen?	☐	☐	☐
♦ Are you talkative, love discussion, and go into lengthy descriptions?	☐	☐	☐
♦ Can you spell better out loud than in writing?	☐	☐	☐

subtotals = _____   _____   _____

x 2   x 1   x 0

totals = _____ + _____ + _____

= _____

KINESTHETIC

	often	sometimes	seldom
♦ Do you speak loudly?	☐	☐	☐
♦ Do you touch people to get their attention?	☐	☐	☐
♦ Do you stand close when talking to someone?	☐	☐	☐
♦ Are you physically oriented and move a lot?	☐	☐	☐
♦ Do you learn by manipulating and doing?	☐	☐	☐
♦ Do you memorize by walking and seeing?	☐	☐	☐
♦ Do you use a finger as a pointer when reading?	☐	☐	☐
♦ Do you gesture a lot?	☐	☐	☐
♦ Do you have difficulty sitting still for long periods?	☐	☐	☐
♦ Do you make decisions based on your feelings?	☐	☐	☐
♦ Do you tap your pen, fingers or foot while listening?	☐	☐	☐
♦ Do you spend time playing sports and physical activities?	☐	☐	☐

subtotals = _____   _____   _____

x 2   x 1   x 0

totals = _____ + _____ + _____

= _____

Fill in the bar graph with your scores.

	V	A	K
24			
23			
22			
21			
20			
19			
18			
17			
16			
15			
14			
13			
12			
11			
10			
9			
8			
7			
6			
5			
4			
3			
2			
1			

GO TO PAGES 4–5 FOR DISCUSSION OF SCORES.

Used by permission of Quantum Learning/SuperCamp, www.quantumlearning.com

Let's find out your learning preference. Are you a VISUAL, AUDITORY, or KINESTHETIC learner, or are you a COMBINATION? First, check the appropriate box for each question. Then, add up your checks going down the column, multiply the total by the number given, and add up the totals for each section. After you have answered the questions for all three sections, use the totals to graph your results.

LEARNING STYLES PROFILE
WHAT TYPE OF LEARNER ARE YOU?

VISUAL – AUDITORY – KINESTHETIC (V-A-K) ASSESSMENT
Mark the appropriate box for each question. Tally your score for each section.

VISUAL

	often	sometimes	seldom
◆ Are you neat and orderly?	☐	☐	☐
◆ Do you speak quickly?	☐	☐	☐
◆ Are you a good long-range planner and organizer?	☐	☐	☐
◆ Are you a good speller and can you actually see the words in your mind?	☐	☐	☐
◆ Do you remember what was seen rather than heard?	☐	☐	☐
◆ Do you memorize by visual association?	☐	☐	☐
◆ Do you have trouble remembering verbal instructions unless they are written down, and do you often ask people to repeat themselves?	☐	☐	☐
◆ Would you rather read than be read to?	☐	☐	☐
◆ Do you doodle during phone conversations/class/meetings?	☐	☐	☐
◆ Would you rather do a demonstration than make a speech?	☐	☐	☐
◆ Do you like art more than music?	☐	☐	☐
◆ Do you know what to say but can't think of the right words?	☐	☐	☐

subtotals = _____ _____ _____

x 2   x 1   x 0

totals = _____ + _____ + _____

= _____

AUDITORY

	often	sometimes	seldom
◆ Do you speak to yourself while working?	☐	☐	☐
◆ Are you easily distracted by noise?	☐	☐	☐
◆ Do you move your lips/pronounce the words as you read?	☐	☐	☐
◆ Do you enjoy reading aloud and listening?	☐	☐	☐
◆ Can you repeat back and mimic tone, pitch, and timbre?	☐	☐	☐
◆ Do you find writing difficult, but are better at telling?	☐	☐	☐
◆ Do you speak in rhythmic patterns?	☐	☐	☐
◆ Do you think you're an eloquent speaker?	☐	☐	☐
◆ Do you like music more than art?	☐	☐	☐
◆ Do you learn by listening and remember what was discussed rather than seen?	☐	☐	☐
◆ Are you talkative, love discussion, and go into lengthy descriptions?	☐	☐	☐
◆ Can you spell better out loud than in writing?	☐	☐	☐

subtotals = _____   _____   _____

$\times 2$ $\times 1$ $\times 0$

totals = _____ + _____ + _____

= _____

KINESTHETIC

	often	sometimes	seldom
◆ Do you speak loudly?	☐	☐	☐
◆ Do you touch people to get their attention?	☐	☐	☐
◆ Do you stand close when talking to someone?	☐	☐	☐
◆ Are you physically oriented and move a lot?	☐	☐	☐
◆ Do you learn by manipulating and doing?	☐	☐	☐
◆ Do you memorize by walking and seeing?	☐	☐	☐
◆ Do you use a finger as a pointer when reading?	☐	☐	☐
◆ Do you gesture a lot?	☐	☐	☐
◆ Do you have difficulty sitting still for long periods?	☐	☐	☐
◆ Do you make decisions based on your feelings?	☐	☐	☐
◆ Do you tap your pen, fingers or foot while listening?	☐	☐	☐
◆ Do you spend time playing sports and physical activities?	☐	☐	☐

subtotals = _____   _____   _____

$\times 2$ $\times 1$ $\times 0$

totals = _____ + _____ + _____

= _____

Fill in the bar graph with your scores.

	V	A	K
24			
23			
22			
21			
20			
19			
18			
17			
16			
15			
14			
13			
12			
11			
10			
9			
8			
7			
6			
5			
4			
3			
2			
1			

GO TO PAGES 4–5 FOR DISCUSSION OF SCORES.

Used by permission of Quantum Learning/SuperCamp, www.quantumlearning.com

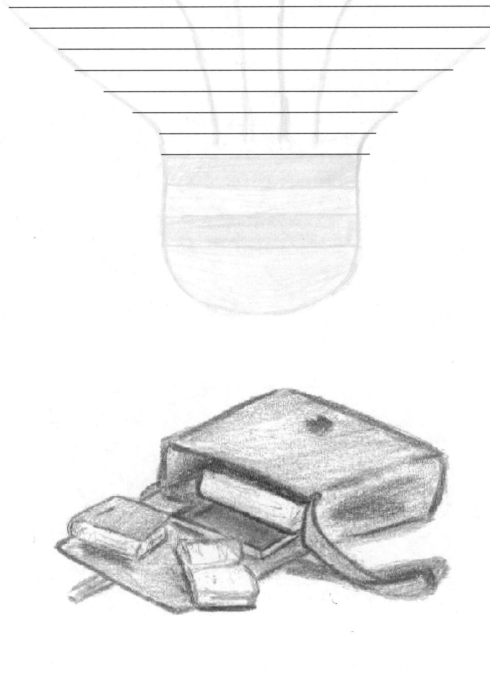

Activity

Here is another great way to gain information
about your unique learning preference(s).

1. Go to *Google* on your computer.
2. Type in the words "learning style preferences."
3. Select an instrument of your choice.
4. Complete the inventory according to their instructions.
5. Print out your score.
6. Below, summarize what you learned about your learning preference.

_____

_____

_____

_____

_____

_____

_____

_____

_____

_____

_____

Activity

Here is another great way to gain information about your unique learning preference(s).

1. Go to *Google* on your computer.
2. Type in the words "learning style preferences."
3. Select an instrument of your choice.
4. Complete the inventory according to their instructions.
5. Print out your score.
6. Below, summarize what you learned about your learning preference.

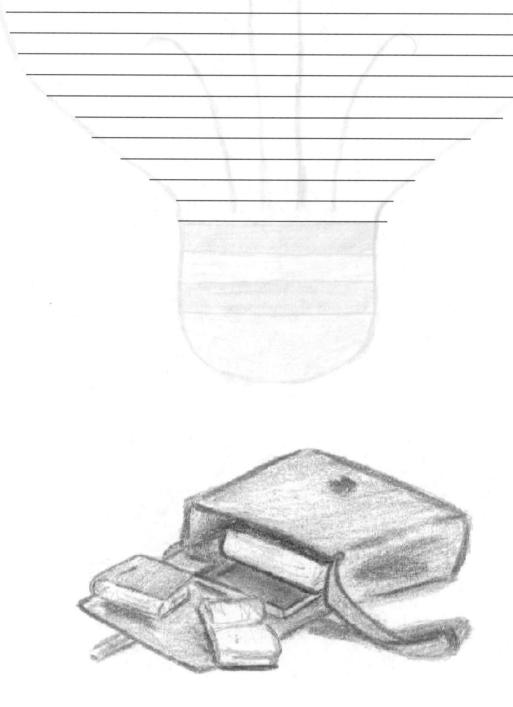

Did you know that intelligence is measured in a variety of ways? Some people are "book smart," "socially smart," "math smart," and "environmentally smart," to name a few. Complete the following survey to see which category encompasses your strengths.

MULTIPLE INTELLIGENCE SURVEY–HOW ARE <u>YOU</u> SMART?
© Walter McKenzie, Surfaquarium Consulting

Part I

Complete each section by placing a "1" next to each statement you feel accurately describes you. If you do not identify with a statement, leave the space blank. Then total the column in each section.

Section 1:

_____ I enjoy categorizing things by common traits.
_____ Ecological issues are important to me.
_____ Hiking and camping are enjoyable activities.
_____ I enjoy working in a garden.
_____ I believe preserving our National Parks is important.
_____ Putting things first in hierarchies makes sense to me.
_____ Animals are important in my life.
_____ My home has a recycling system in place.
_____ I enjoy studying biology, botany, and/or zoology.
_____ I spend a great deal of time outdoors.

_____ = TOTAL for Section 1

Section 2:

_____ I easily pick up on patterns.
_____ I focus in on noise and sounds.
_____ Moving to a beat is easy for me.
_____ I've always been interested in playing an instrument.
_____ The cadence of poetry intrigues me.
_____ I remember things by putting them in a rhyme.
_____ Concentration is difficult while listening to a radio or television.
_____ I enjoy many kinds of music.
_____ Musicals are more interesting than dramatic plays.
_____ Remembering song lyrics is easy for me.

_____ = TOTAL for Section 2

Section 3:

_____ I keep my things neat and orderly.

_____ Step-by-step directions are a big help.

_____ Solving problems comes easily to me.

_____ I get easily frustrated with disorganized people.

_____ I can complete calculations quickly in my head.

_____ Puzzles requiring reasoning are fun.

_____ I can't begin an assignment until all my questions are answered.

_____ Structures help me be successful.

_____ I find working on a computer spreadsheet or database rewarding.

_____ Things have to make sense to me or I am dissatisfied.

_____ = TOTAL for Section 3

Section 4:

_____ It is important to see my role in the "big picture" of things.

_____ I enjoy discussing questions about life.

_____ Religion is important to me.

_____ I enjoy viewing art masterpieces.

_____ Relaxation and meditation exercises are rewarding.

_____ I like visiting breathtaking sites in nature.

_____ I enjoy reading ancient and modern philosophers.

_____ Learning new things is easier when I understand their value.

_____ I wonder if there are other forms of intelligent life in the universe.

_____ Studying history and ancient culture helps give me perspective.

_____ = TOTAL for Section 4

Section 5:

_____ I learn best interacting with others.

_____ The more the merrier!

_____ Study groups are very productive for me.

_____ I enjoy chat rooms.

_____ Participating in politics is important.

_____ Television and radio talk shows are enjoyable.

_____ I am a "team player."

_____ I dislike working alone.

_____ Clubs and extracurricular activities are fun.

_____ I pay attention to social issues and causes.

_____ = TOTAL for Section 5

Section 6:

____ I enjoy making things with my hands.

____ Sitting still for long periods of time is difficult for me.

____ I enjoy outdoor games and sports.

____ I value non-verbal communication, such as sign language.

____ A fit body is important for a fit mind.

____ Arts and crafts are enjoyable pastimes.

____ Expression through dance is beautiful.

____ I like working with tools.

____ I live an active lifestyle.

____ I learn by doing.

____ = TOTAL for Section 6

Section 7:

____ I enjoy reading all kinds of materials.

____ Taking notes helps me remember and understand.

____ I faithfully contact friends through letters and/or e-mail.

____ It is easy for me to explain my ideas to others.

____ I keep a journal.

____ Word puzzles like crosswords and jumbles are fun.

____ I write for pleasure.

____ I enjoy playing with words like puns, anagrams, and spoonerisms.

____ Foreign languages interest me.

____ Debates and public speaking are activities in which I like to participate.

____ = TOTAL for Section 7

Section 8:

____ I am keenly aware of my moral beliefs.

____ I learn best when I have an emotional attachment to the subject.

____ Fairness is important to me.

____ My attitude effects how I learn.

____ Social justice issues concern me.

____ Working alone can be just as productive as working in a group.

____ I need to know why I should do something before I agree to do it.

____ When I believe in something I will give 100% effort to it.

____ I like to be involved in causes that help others.

____ I am willing to protest or sign a petition to right a wrong.

____ = TOTAL for Section 8

Section 9:

____ I can imagine ideas in my mind.

____ Rearranging a room is fun for me.

____ I enjoy creating art using varied media.

____ I remember well using graphic organizers.

____ Performance art can be very gratifying.

____ Spreadsheets are great for making charts, graphs, and tables.

____ Three dimensional puzzles bring me much enjoyment.

____ Music videos are very stimulating.

____ I can recall things in mental pictures.

____ I am good at reading maps and blueprints.

____ = TOTAL for Section 9

Part II

Using this chart, record your totals from each section and multiply each total by 10.

Section	Total	Multiply	Score
1		x10	
2		x10	
3		x10	
4		x10	
5		x10	
6		x10	
7		x10	
8		x10	
9		x10	

Part III
Plot your scores on the bar graph provided.

100									
90									
80									
70									
60									
50									
40									
30									
20									
10									
0	Sec 1	Sec 2	Sec 3	Sec 4	Sec 5	Sec 6	Sec 7	Sec 8	Sec 9

Part IV
Find your strength below and then **look up it's definition** in the **glossary**.

Key:

Section 1 – This reflects your NATURALIST strength.
Section 2 – This suggests your MUSICAL strength.
Section 3 – This indicates your LOGICAL strength.
Section 4 – This illustrates your EXISTENTIAL strength.
Section 5 – This shows your INTERPERSONAL strength.
Section 6 – This tells your KINESTHETIC strength.
Section 7 – This indicates your VERBAL strength.
Section 8 – This reflects your INTRAPERSONAL strength.
Section 9 – This suggests your VISUAL strength.

REMEMBER:
☺ Everyone possesses, to some degree, all the intelligences!
☺ You can strengthen an intelligence!
☺ This survey is meant as a snapshot in time – it can and will change!
☺ Knowing your Multiple Intelligence strengths are meant to empower, not label!

Permission to reprint from © Walter McKenzie, Surfaquarium Consulting, http://surfaquarium.com/mi.htm), 1999.

Your learning profile will provide insights into how you prefer to study. Complete the profile below to determine your learning preferences. Check each statement that you <u>strongly believe</u> is true for you. Leave the <u>others blank</u>. Then add up the number of checks in each section.

MY LEARNING PROFILE

Sound
Some people like Bach, some people like boom.
Some people have to study where it's silent as a tomb.
Do you need noise? Do you need quiet?
How will you know? You'll know if you try it.

☐ When I study I prefer quiet!
☐ Traffic, music, the TV, airplanes, and talking keep me from concentrating.
☐ People or other students who move, squirm, erase papers, tap with their feet, or pencil, or ruler really bother me when I'm studying or reading.
☐ Sometimes I have to cover my ears with my hands so that I can concentrate on what I am studying.

Number of checks:____ (1A)

☐ When I study I prefer to do it with music.
☐ I just can't concentrate when the room is absolutely quiet.
☐ I feel comfortable when the TV or stereo is on when I study.
☐ When I do my homework or read, I like to be in a place where other people are talking and working.

Number of checks:____ (1B)

Light
Eyes that squint or open and strain –
When the light is wrong there is no gain.
Turn the light way up! Turn the light down low!
When the light is right, I'm ready to go.

☐ When I study I put on all the lights.
☐ I like to read or do homework outdoors.
☐ I often get sleepy or can't concentrate unless I have on bright lights.
☐ I always move to the windows or under large banks of light when I study.

Number of checks:____ (2A)

☐ I prefer to read in low or very dim light.
☐ I like to do homework with most of the lights off.
☐ I like to use just one small lamp when I do my homework.
☐ I can read under tables and in dark corners.

Number of checks:____ (2B)

Temperature

The wrong degree of heat inside
Can make those facts just slip and slide.
Some like it warm, some like it cool—
The temp in the room is a learning tool.

☐ I prefer the warmer weather school months.
☐ I study best in a warm room.
☐ I usually wear sweaters or extra clothes indoors.
☐ I often feel too cold and prefer the heat on when I do homework.   Number of checks:____ (3A)

☐ I prefer the cooler weather school months.
☐ I prefer it to be cool when I study.
☐ I don't wear sweaters and extra clothes indoors; they make me feel too warm.
☐ I often feel too warm, and I like the heat off when I do homework.   Number of checks:____ (3B)

Setting

These chairs of wood or seats of plastic
Make me squirm and really spastic.
They don't help my mind to grow.
What I really need is soft and low.

☐ I prefer to do homework at a table or desk.
☐ I get sleepy or lazy if I try to read on a bed or couch.
☐ I like to sit up straight when I study or write.
☐ I just can't concentrate if I lie down or stretch out when I study.   Number of checks:____ (4A)

☐ I like to sit on a soft chair or couch when I study.
☐ I can't concentrate too well when I sit at a desk or table.
☐ I often read on the floor.
☐ Sometimes I work on my bed or stretched out on a couch.   Number of checks:____ (4B)

Self

Learning by myself is what suits me,
Like a strong proud eagle flying free.
No one to hurry, no one to race—
Just going along at my own pace.

☐ I really like to work by myself.
☐ I usually don't prefer to work in groups.
☐ I do work best by myself!
☐ Don't send someone to help me.   Number of checks:____ (5A)

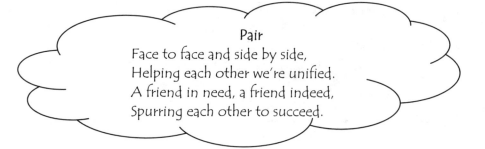

Pair
Face to face and side by side,
Helping each other we're unified.
A friend in need, a friend indeed,
Spurring each other to succeed.

☐ I prefer to study with one person.
☐ I get more done when I have a partner.
☐ I learn more if I can ask questions of a friend and we talk about it.
☐ I like to describe what I'm learning to a partner.　　Number of checks:____ (5B)

Team
Studying with others in a team or loop,
All tasks are a snap in a working group.
We all chip in and even have fun,
But we keep going 'til the job is done.

☐ It's fun to work on a project with friends.
☐ I prefer to work with a team or committee.
☐ We all help each other in a group.
☐ I need several people to talk about things so I understand what to learn.
　　　　　　　　　　　　　　　Number of checks:____ (5C)

Adult
Taking my questions to adults
Gives me the answers for best results.
Reality check—adult perspective
Makes my learning more effective.

☐ I need the teacher to show me how to do things.
☐ I like it when the teacher checks my work.
☐ I like to work with the teacher, my parents, or an adult when I'm alone with one of them.
☐ I prefer to discuss things with an adult.
　　　　　　　　　　　　Number of checks:____ (5D)

Varied

Some people like a change of scene,
Some people need the same routine
For learning things the same old way.
While others change from day to day.

- ☐ Sometimes I like to work alone or with a friend or the teacher.
- ☐ I like to work with different people.
- ☐ I like to do my assignments in different ways, alone and with others.
- ☐ When we work in groups I like different ways of doing things.

Number of checks:____ (5E)

Senses

Do you SEE what I mean?
Do you HEAR what I say?
Are you getting in TOUCH?
Are you MOVING my way?
What's your preference?
How do you learn?
You can learn it all
It is your turn.

Seeing pictures

- ☐ I can really learn it if I see it on TV or in a movie.
- ☐ I like computer programs with pictures.
- ☐ I like to read books with diagrams and pictures.
- ☐ I like to sketch, underline, and use colors or my own symbols when I take notes.

Number of checks:____ (6A)

Seeing words

- ☐ I learn best if I read about it.
- ☐ I like computer programs with lots of words.
- ☐ I prefer assignments with clear directions in words I understand.
- ☐ I like word games like Scrabble™.

Number of checks:____(6B)

Listening

- ☐ I learn best when I hear the teacher explain something.
- ☐ I can learn by listening to audio tape.
- ☐ I remember things best when I talk about them with someone.
- ☐ I can remember things when someone reads them to me.

Number of checks:____(6C)

Touching

- ☐ I learn best with puzzles and games.
- ☐ I like to make and build things.
- ☐ I really enjoy working with my hands.
- ☐ I prefer learning material that I can touch and move.

Number of checks:____(6D)

Doing/moving

- ☐ I like homework assignments that ask me to do things away from school.
- ☐ I like charades, games, and projects where I do things and have to move.
- ☐ I prefer learning something by acting, role-playing, interviewing, reporting, by getting all of me involved.
- ☐ Field trips help me to understand what I'm learning in school.

Number of checks:____(6E)

98

> **Time of day**
>
> In the morning, my blood doesn't flow,
> My brain is slow, can't get up and go.
> I rise with the sun, I'll rest later
> 'Cause in the evening I'm a couch potato.

Morning:
- ☐ I remember things better in early classes of the day.
- ☐ Usually I like to get up between 6 a.m. and 8 a.m.
- ☐ I wish I could take classes beginning no later than 8 a.m.
- ☐ I would like to begin school early and end before 2 o'clock.

Number of checks:____ (7A)

Mid-day:
- ☐ Usually I like to get up between 8 a.m. and 10 a.m.
- ☐ I start to come alive after 10 a.m.
- ☐ I wish I could study the most difficult subjects just before lunch.
- ☐ I like to work with teachers or other students in the late morning.

Number of checks:____ (7B)

Afternoon:
- ☐ I wish school would begin after lunch.
- ☐ I like to do my homework right after I get home from school.
- ☐ I'm most alert toward the end of the school day.
- ☐ I wish I could take my most difficult classes between 1 p.m. and 4 p.m.

Number of checks:____ (7C)

Evening:
- ☐ I like to stay up late to do my homework.
- ☐ I feel wide awake when I'm supposed to go to sleep.
- ☐ I wish school would start at night.
- ☐ I would like to work on school assignments with teachers or other students after 8 p.m.

Number of checks:____ (7D)

Fill in the number of responses for each section.
4 checks = strong preference, 3 checks = preference

sound:
(1A) Quiet ____
(1B) Sound ____

lights:
(2A) Bright ____
(2B) Dim/soft ____

temperature:
(3A) Warm ____
(3B) Cool ____

setting:
(4A) Formal ____
(4B) Informal ____

learning groups:
(5A) Self ____
(5D) Adult ____

(5B) Pair ____
(5E) Varied ____

(5C) Team ____

senses:
(6A) Seeing Pictures ____
(6B) Seeing Words ____
(6C) Listening ____
(6D) Touching ____
(6E) Doing/Moving ____

time of day:
(7A) Morning ____
(7B) Mid-Day ____
(7C) Afternoon ____
(7D) Evening ____

Used by permission of Quantum Learning/SuperCamp, www.quantumlearning.com

Activity – AN ONLINE INVENTORY
STUDY SKILLS CHECKLIST:

1. Go to the following web-site: http://www.ucc.vt.edu
   The purpose of this inventory is to discover information about your own **study habits and attitudes**.

2. Scroll down the list and click on "Study Skills Self-Help Info." See list.

3. At the end of the page, click "Study Skills Inventory" icon. This will send you to pages on the web-site for help with scheduling, concentration, listening and note-taking, reading, exams, and writing skills. If you answered one "yes" or all "no"s in any of the categories you are probably proficient enough in that area. You may still want to read through the suggestions in areas that interest you.

4. <u>Write</u> a 5-7 sentence paragraph summarizing your strengths and weaknesses and some strategies to improve.

5. For more activities on this site, click on any of the five categories under "Online Study Skills Workshops."

_____
_____
_____
_____
_____
_____
_____
_____
_____
_____
_____
_____
_____
_____
_____
_____
_____

For another site with inventories and more information on brain-based learning: www.gigglepotz.com/mistudent.htm
Scroll and click on "Student Questionaire." Take the test and score results.

For information on your learning style after you have taken one or both of the assessments, see pages 4 and 5 of this handbook.

Let's see how you would evaluate yourself on your study skills before we go any further.

STUDY SKILLS SURVEY

Read the following statements to assess how competent you feel at this point in your educational career with regards to study skills. Check those that apply to you and tally your marks. A total of 10 would mean you feel you have mastered that skill; a 5 would mean you are somewhat competent, and a 1 would mean you lack that skill. BE HONEST WITH YOURSELF!! Honest self-assessment is a vital part of learning.

1. ❑ I am able to set realistic academic and personal goals.
2. ❑ I understand how I learn best.
3. ❑ I am able to manage my time to meet school, activity, and relaxation needs.
4. ❑ As I read my textbooks, I am able to learn what is essential for the class.
5. ❑ I am able to stay alert and focused during class.
6. ❑ I take lecture notes that are complete, clear, and useful.
7. ❑ I am able to listen effectively to get the most out of class discussions.
8. ❑ I use a variety of strategies to remember information.
9. ❑ I know what type of study space I need in order to do my work well.
10. ❑ I can differentiate between essential and non-essential information in class discussions.
11. ❑ I can differentiate between essential and non-essential information in my textbook readings.
12. ❑ I am able to motivate myself to study.
13. ❑ I am able to stay on top of my course work.
14. ❑ I am good at testing myself to see if I really understand information.
15. ❑ I am able to study course materials so that I understand and can retain information for exams.
16. ❑ I study effectively for exams.
17. ❑ I take exams in an efficient and systematic manner ("Study Skills Survey" 1).

Activity

Use the lines below and on the next page to discuss what areas you would like to learn about in order to improve your academic success during the school year. You may also want to reflect on what you have learned about yourself as a whole after taking one or more of these inventories.

_____
_____
_____

PARENT/TEACHER ADDENDUM

The *Study Skills Tool Kit* is a carefully crafted resource for your child/student. We thoughtfully organized its contents in a logical order to: (1) guide and generate your (and the student's) understanding of learning preferences and (2) enhance classroom study/life skills. One of the many benefits of this resource is that you can use it over and over again during the academic career — it is designed to be revisited.

Here are some suggestions on how to use the workbook:

➢ The Table of Contents outlines the 10 major sections of the *Study Skills Tool Kit*. While each section of this booklet contains excellent information for all learners and educators, the Table of Contents helps you to easily find the information you are looking for. Note that this section is also color-coded to correspond to the pages. You do not necessarily need to follow the order of this Table of Contents as you go through the book.

➢ First and foremost, it is strongly recommended that you determine the learning style of each student. Go to the "How Do You Learn?" section first and tackle the "Learning Styles Profile."

➢ Revisit often the surveys and instruments to reassess a student's learning style. This process should occur at least once a year or each semester. Additional copies of the surveys and instruments can be found on pages 81-100.

➢ Each year have students choose only one color for a highlighter and/or pen to use each as they mark or write in the book. The following year, the students can choose a different color.

➢ Expand upon sections as needed. Bring in additional recommended written resources and/or websites. Expand upon "Activities" and "Reflections." Seek student input for additional activities.

➢ Revisit sections of the book to reinforce skills (i.e. highlighting or note-taking).

➢ For additional information on instruments, surveys and/or principles (i.e. "Keys of Excellence"), visit particular websites and/or written resources. Our Works Cited page is a great resource to find additional information regarding topics contained in the *Study Skills Tool Kit*. (Note: The Works Cited page is also an example of the MLA style of documentation to use as an example in the section on writing papers.)

➢ Have students use the "Notes" pages to make individual comments, questions, or for journal writing.

➢ Use various content areas as examples to reinforce study strategies in each section (i.e. a science book to reinforce highlighting).

➢ Always teach something new at least four times before trying something else. Students should use a new study strategy four times before scrapping it or moving on to a new strategy.